MAKING
THE DECISION

REBOOT YOUR LIFE IN 90 DAYS

This book is guaranteed to get your life "UN-STUCK!"

Jan M. Newby, Author of The Pocket Financial Planner

Foreword by Dr. Nathaniel J. Williams

Making the Decision

Executive Editor: Angela Bell
Assistant Editor: Ashley Baity
Editor-In-Chief: J. M. Newby
Editorial Team
Cover Designer: © Tim Feather / 110 Front Communications
Printer: Central Imaging and Printing

Newby, J. M.

Making the Decision: Reboot Your Life In 90 Days
-    Jan M. Newby – 1st ed.

ISBN: 978-0-981-47428-1

Send all inquiries to:
Appleseed Professional Development, LLC
appleseedpd@yahoo.com
Eastpointe, MI 48021

To Brandén a brilliant aspiring "great decision maker!"

Always remember every decision you make has
the ability to determine results you desire, or create
regrets you will reluctantly acquire.

- J. M. Newby

DECISIONS... DECISIONS... DECISIONS...

- Do you ever wonder what your life would look like if you could rewind your life 5 years?

- What would you have done differently, that you believe would put you in a different position, than where you are today?

- Do you sometimes wish that you had the opportunity to retract some of the risky investments you made?

- Have you ever sat down and thought about the many times you started the year out with fitness goals or diets that you failed at after only 1-month?

- Do you wish you had more time to spend with family, friends or build fulfilling healthy relationships?

- Have you ever had an opportunity to establish a good networking possibility, but because of fears you may have had, you did not pursue it?

- How many goals have you created over the last three years that you gave up on only after the first 12-months?

- Do you think about how much easier life would seem if you had more time to relax, meditate and simply enjoy the good life you've always desired?

- Do you ever wish you would have spent more time praying about a matter, before making a final decision?

- Do you desire to de-clutter "stuck" places in your life and establish balance in your decision making process, so you can end each day with results instead of regrets?

"Making the Decision to Reboot Your Life" is your answer to help you start flourishing right where you are…

Making The Decision

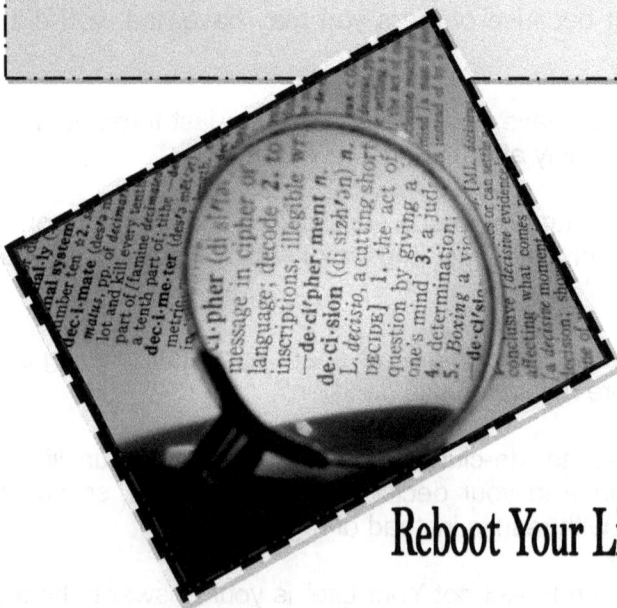

Reboot Your Life In 90 Days!

PREFACE

What a great day to start thinking about making a decision, a decision so impactful, that in just 12 weeks from today you may very well change the full course of the rest of your life. If you are reading this preface, it is assumed that somehow you or someone you know obtained this extraordinary book on the sole premise that the decision to create change in your life is desired.

"Making The Decision" was designed specifically with you in mind, within these pages you will begin to evaluate how you currently arrived at the place you are in right now in your life. Then, you will be given an opportunity to strategically learn how to master six-core major life areas to obtain change and create a total life balance. We will assess physical make-up, financial plans, social interaction, spiritual enrichment, goals established and how you manage your time.

The term soul-searching is something we will use as an initial strategy to create blueprints of your life. Your blueprints will help you take a thorough examination of your thinking, feelings and current undertakings. Being completely honest is imperative in order to bring to light every intricate detail about emotions, ulterior thoughts, what motivates you, brings discouragement, contentment with a "I've done enough" attitude or give-up mentality, and/or cause of a continuous digress to being what we will call simply "stuck."

If we are not producing fruitful results in our daily lives, then we are stuck or held up in an immovable position. When we get to the place of "stuck" at any given time, we must learn to stop what we're doing, evaluate where we are, re-evaluate where we need to be, grasp hold of a solution and/or direction of what it will take for us to keep moving forward.

When it comes to something as serious as making a decision about life matters, that we desire to create change in, then it is time to literally get **CONTROL** . . . of our situation, **ALT(ER)** . . . our routine, centralize the problem, and click the **DELETE** . . . button on the areas of hindrance. Hence we will then find the solutions we need in order to **RE-BOOT** and start back over again, towards an abundant flow of direction!

Over the next 90-days of your life, you will discover if you are a good goal planner or procrastinator, if you successfully manage your time and what your physical, mental, spiritual and financial appetite may be. You will then have the opportunity to discover how you can better digest these life concerns on a daily basis after you "Re-Boot."

We are what and who we have created ourselves into being thus far in our lives. If you are not completely satisfied with every area of your life or how you handle daily life endeavors, then in order to experience change, make the decision to take a leap of faith. Follow the plan of action contained in this book, and we guarantee it will be a decision worth making.

I have been taught and stand on the belief as a Teacher that a good Teacher must lend himself to the lesson. It may be easy to coach someone, but it is much more rewarding if you can incorporate self-experience within the instruction. In order to tell a true story of success the Teacher should have passed the test first.

Before completing this book, I along with several other courageous persons agreed to take the 90-Day challenge of self-examination in that of our own lives. The desired outcome was to discover how we can live a more abundant life. Results achieved were a more dedicated prayer life, financial abundance, physical weight-loss, better goal-setter and planner, improved time-management, and leverage obtained in social interaction and relationships.

I am overwhelmingly grateful to all the persons that agreed to take the plunge with me and launch off into the deep. We all made it to the other side without a shipwreck, it was a great experience. I am excited about the success you also will achieve from implementing and mastering the strategies throughout your exploit of "Making the Decision to Re-Boot Your Life in 90 Days!"

- - -

MAKING
THE DECISION

To Find Balance In Your Life

REBOOT YOUR LIFE IN 90 DAYS

CONTENTS

INTRODUCTION

DECISION MAKERS ARE TRUE CHAMPIONS

"The race is not to the swift, nor the battle to the strong, neither yet bread to the wise, nor yet riches to men of understanding, nor yet favour to men of skill; but time and chance happeneth to them all." – Ecclesiastes 9:11 KJV

True champions work hard to achieve their desired goals of success. Happiness will derive out of the success accomplished, but after all the accolades are given, wisdom in learning how to handle success will far exceed beyond the actual medal obtained. Wisdom must be used when it comes to staying humble, and keeping a determined mind-set to never settle for just one win. Continual stride towards the mark for a much valuable prize is what life should accumulate to.

A true winner always reaches for higher heights in order to stay on track to meeting every goal. In a pursuit of life goals, a foundation of hard work would seem to pay off, but of course suddenly at any given moment the unexpected could happen: "Life." An individual that see their end from the beginning should always incorporate the possibility of bumps in the road, pot holes on the track, or a necessary need to stop for refresher breaks. Planning for changes or unexpected jams, will allow the true winner to re-set their course, and re-boot their navigation, in order to finish the race. Time and chance are essentially unpredictable, and that is emphatically the very reason that wisdom must always be at the forefront of determining the next best decision.

The first thing we think about when making a decision is the difficult notion that we are now expected to choose, with a firm, clear-cut response to something we are faced with, without any time to hesitate or delay.

Well, the process of coming to a conclusion or determination about something is exactly just that: "Making a Decision". Suddenly, we may cringe at the very thought, step back, want to put it out of our mind, suppress the possibility or at worst, just pass the responsibility on to someone else, that we believe will be more capable of helping us to make up our mind. "Are you listening to the over exaggeration in your mental word processor?"

STOP. . . Get a hold of yourself! Literally! Take hold of the reigns of your mind, and begin to re-direct your thoughts. You sincerely hold within, the power to dominant and influence how you will live out the rest of your life from this very moment. The process starts in your mind, if you ever have fruitful thoughts of being successful, then surely you have the ability to imagine what your life could be like in just 90-Days from today.

Yesterday has passed, today give yourself a "present" of victory, and focus your thoughts on the possibilities of the many gifts that tomorrow can bring you. When you are presented with a wrapped gift, more times than none, you instantaneously have an anticipation of what is contained inside. Rarely, have I met anyone, who does not appreciate when someone gives them something, especially when they least expect it. If you have read thus far, within this book, you hold a gift in your hands, and an opportunity to discover an unexpected gift for a renewed transformed way of living. Take ownership of the gift given; open up your mind to change, be courageous enough to desire a champion attitude.

Hope of change is accredited to an individual choice, envision and embrace a life of anticipated possibilities of success. Once you embark upon a new way of living, and you begin to understand the gifts and talents uniquely purposed for your life, you will have the opportunity to think of how you can share your knowledge with someone else. Making a decision to live a life of abundance is learning the value of planting seeds.

If you have run the race of life for any length of time, and never took the initiative to impart or plant seeds into the life of someone else, begin to consider what truly is the core purpose and meaning of living. When you live a purposed filled life you should also aspire to have your life carry on through ensuring that you plant seeds that will have the ability to develop and continuously grow. A true champion decision maker will confidently desire to share life strengths, experience and knowledge they possess with others, in order to produce a winning harvest.

After 90-days if you do not experience complete transformation in your life, then you strayed somewhere along the course of plans. You must stay the full course of the track, be consistent, diligent, and get serious about what goals you can achieve in the end. Ninety days is only twelve weeks, two-thousand sixty hours, and well worth a lifetime of living in abundance. We will make it to the finish line, you and me both.

Ready - Set - Go!

FOREWORD

Making change in your life is an extremely difficult task because it requires you to manage the three stages of change: the beginning, the middle, and the end. If you only had to manage one of these stages, you could be successful with relative ease. It is the attempt to bring it all together "under one roof" that leads to the fits and starts of the change process. Jan Newby understands this principle and has authored a book to explain what is needed to begin this process: "Making the Decision to Reboot Your Life in 90 days."

At first glance, 90 days might seem like a long time. However, in the larger scheme of things, it is a short period to invest in yourself and your future. As you are already reading this, you are on your way to change already. I want to encourage you not to give up. Recognize that these 90 days have a beginning — today — and that they will have a middle in the 88 days to follow, as well as an end on the 90th day.

I sincerely hope that after embarking on this process of change and improvement, you will be motivated to continue, as Ms. Newby suggest, in order "to find balance in your life." Your path will not be easy, but the rewards will be as plentiful and deserved. Change is a journey, not a destination. I wish you the very best in your first steps toward your personal best and obtaining your desired results.

Dr. Nathaniel J. Williams
www.drnatwilliams.com

HOW THE 90-DAY RE-BOOT SYSTEM WILL WORK FOR YOU

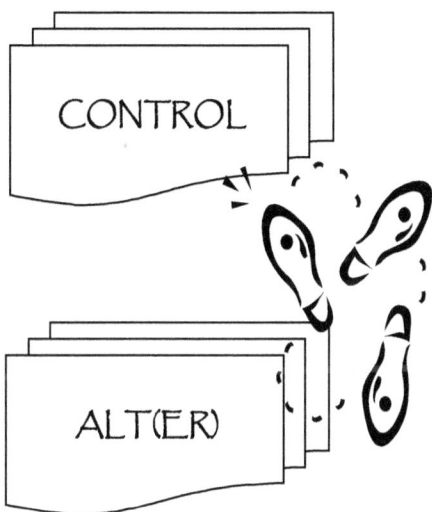

CONTROL

ALT(ER)

DELETE

RE-BOOT

Step 1

Decide to initiate a process to take control of every area of your life you are currently dissatisfied with. This step is positioning you to acknowledge that you have power to create change.

Step 2

After you have decided that there is a need for change in a situation you are faced with, then you will feel empowered to modify or re-evaluate steps to determining a possible solution.

Step 3

Strategizing a method to move beyond recognizable hindrances is a wise decision. However, once you do, it is imperative to literally detach or pull out the roots, so that you will not be tempted to re-visit the same place again, that has the ultimate ability to creating further limitations or distractions.

Step 4

Once you have challenged yourself to courageously go beyond the borders of your own limitations, and completely remove all distractions, you will discover what living a life in abundance is all about. You will experience a lifestyle with more than adequate and overflowing resources.

THE DECISION MAKING
SYSTEMATIC STRUCTURE

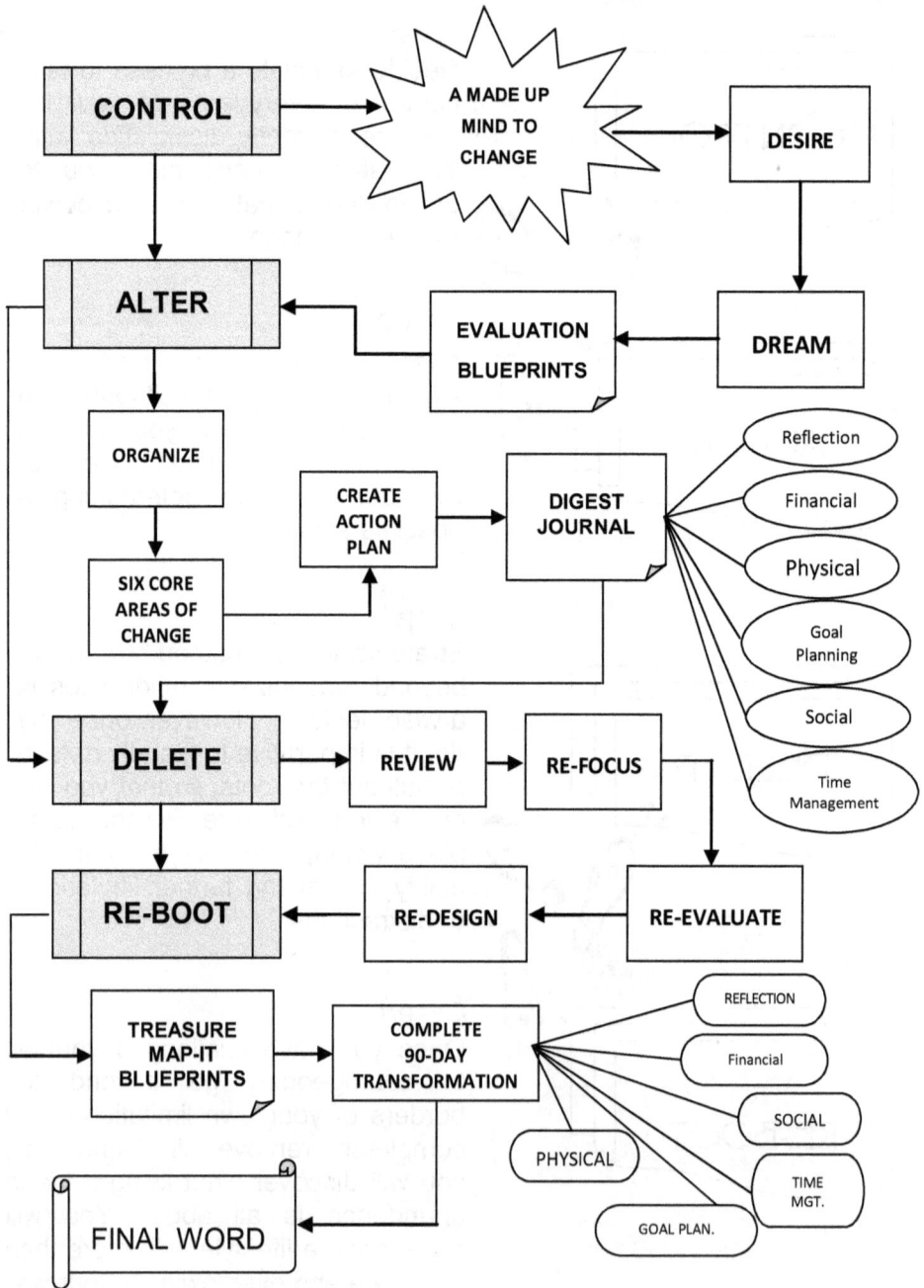

CONTROL → A MADE UP MIND TO CHANGE → **DESIRE**

ALTER ← EVALUATION BLUEPRINTS ← **DREAM**

ORGANIZE

CREATE ACTION PLAN → **DIGEST JOURNAL**

SIX CORE AREAS OF CHANGE

- Reflection
- Financial
- Physical
- Goal Planning
- Social
- Time Management

DELETE → REVIEW → RE-FOCUS

RE-BOOT ← RE-DESIGN ← RE-EVALUATE

TREASURE MAP-IT BLUEPRINTS → COMPLETE 90-DAY TRANSFORMATION

- REFLECTION
- Financial
- SOCIAL
- PHYSICAL
- TIME MGT.
- GOAL PLAN.

FINAL WORD

COMMITMENT

"For we walk by faith, not by sight" – II Corinthians 5:7 KJV

It is always easy to take a path that appears to be shorter or the least complicated to follow, as opposed to a path with opposition. Making the decision to reboot your life will be a faith walk; it is going to take focus and unwavering commitment. When you make a commitment to something you ultimately are choosing to devote time, energy and become obligated to the task at hand.

If you are able to put in the amount of responsibility and loyalty that it would take to create change in your life you will find that it will also take work. As you work through breaking down barriers of old habits, determine that you will not allow fear of failure to distract you or discourage you from walking through a path that will lead you to abundant living.

Besides having faith, your entire mindset will cause you to ultimately change your behavior and the way you see things in your path. One pathway may only require you to use a flash light to get you pass hindering areas, while the other requires faith to lead you into new territories of living. One way makes us responsible for being courageous enough to figure out the path we should take, while the other may present us with familiar territories so we will just be content and stay where we are.

Which road will you take?

Will you let fear of the unknown keep you from stepping out of your comfort zone? Or will you have faith to believe, that the right path will simply require commitment regardless of opposition?

The 90 Day Commitment

90 DAY COMMITMENT & PETITION

I _____, this _____ day of _____, in the year of _____ commit to enhancing my life through truthfully documenting my current lifestyle decision-making process focusing on six core areas: Spiritually, Financially, Physically, Socially, Time Management and Goal Planning. I will take time to re-evaluate necessary areas of development, with the expectation of *Making The Decision* to implement new strategies, in order to completely *Reboot My Life In 90 Days*, and experience a life of abundant living.

Signed,

_____
Your Signature

As a further demonstration of your commitment, I agree to submit my testimonial to: Appleseed Professional Development, LLC at www.appleseedpd.com or email at appleseedpd@yahoo.com, to commemorate my achievement. A congratulatory certificate will be sent to you, to show our applause in your dedication and determination to experience a life full of abundance.

BALANCING LIFE
NOTABLE KEY PRINCIPLES

How can you win the game of balancing all your daily life endeavors? A balanced life may sometimes seem like weights on a scale. Weights can be burdensome, heavy, and 'down-right' nagging at times. However, if you take a moment to objectively look at how you can control thoughtful moves, you will master the ability of transforming heavy weights of regrets to light weights of results that will not weigh you down, but instead build you up. When you train your mindset how to handle light weights of daily life matters in moderation, you are inevitably building continuous momentum towards achieving desirable results from decisions you make.

At any given time in your decision making process, like weights on a scale one extra weight of life-matter has the ability to weigh one way or the other. Life-matter can be taking a chance in game playing, you can choose to be a wise decision maker and make things happen: causing the scale to lean towards your desired result, or you can take a chance and procrastinate causing another move to be made whether you agree or not, ending the game with regret. Take time before playing the balancing game of life-matters to incorporate the following notable key principles into your daily life regime, so you can be a conqueror everyday:

Key #1: Pray often and always so that your faith will exceed your ability.

Key #2: Diligently work-daily towards goals and aspirations!

Key #3: Visualize a successful ending from the beginning.

Key #4: Plan, evaluate, review, create objectives, and make good observations.

Key #5: Master the six-core areas of total well being.

Key #6: Create a consistent checks & balance system for everyday life matters.

Balancing Life Notable Key Principles – Continued

Key #7: Maintain an attitude of self-assurance in knowing your life's purpose.

Key #8 : Prepare a realistic navigation process and you will avoid many obstacles along the way.

Key #9: Stay motivated, encouraged and determined to excel beyond your greatest expectations.

Key #10: When you have done your very best, stretch to do even better.

Key #11: Believe you are the greatest success story ever designed.

Key #12: Train your ear to hear, eyes to see, and mind to contain fruitful life accomplishments.

Golden Key
Establishing a successful balanced lifestyle is a lifetime achievement!

— — —

CONTROL

Get serious about unlocking and taking control
of every blocked area in your life. . .

Day: 1~7

CONTROL

Control is the power to direct or determine an outcome.
- ***Restraint:*** *discipline in personal and social activities*
- ***Operate:*** *handle and cause to function*
- ***Command or Mastery***

Within the coming days, you will have the opportunity to blueprint actual life events you partake in on a daily basis. Based on what you document, you will obtain a good indication of areas you spend most of your time, and discover a core area that all your current life endeavors derive from. Most importantly, you should see a pattern of how you make decisions or determine certain outcomes pertaining to everyday living.

Areas of your life that cause you to stay in an unproductive state or you have deemed unsatisfactory, is reason enough to desire taking control over and creating plans to implement change. Many times we habitually handle daily matters over extensive periods of time without ever thinking there is an actual problem developing, such as procrastination or time management issues, lack of organization or financial management.

How can you begin to control areas of your life that you believe are stagnate or unproductive? You begin to make decisions to harness ownership of what you have control over, and what you do not. Once you determine that you are ready to obtain better control in areas of your life that have simply gotten a little out of control, it is imperative to re-direct your thinking and behavioral patterns when making future decisions.

You have the ability to either choose to make things happen in your life, as opposed to simply just allowing life to happen. When you learn how to discipline your thoughts, you will develop a results-oriented mindset, and ultimately achieve end results on any given situation that you desire. Practicing and incorporating discipline in your daily life choices will allow you to produce well-thought out plans where you will not regret choices you make.

In order to operate in a more disciplined manner when handling personal or social life endeavors you must begin to command and declare what you desire your outcome of any situation to be.

TAKING CONTROL

Document concerns in your life that require you to take control.

What areas in your life do you have control over?

_____

_____

_____

_____

_____

_____

_____

_____

_____

_____

What areas of your life do you know you do not have control over?

_____

_____

_____

_____

_____

_____

_____

_____

_____

What areas in your life do you have the power to re-direct or
determine a different outcome?

_____

_____

_____

_____

_____

_____

_____

MADE UP MIND

#1
Pray often and always so that your faith will exceed your ability.

Continuing to do the same things, the same way and expect different results is defined as a form of insanity.

Making a decision to change from a habitual way of doing something, may not be easy. Many times you can start off well in your change of direction, until you get to a pressure point, or hot spot of challenging circumstances, that may cause you to fall short. "Making the Decision to Re-boot Your Life in just 90 days," will expose you to powerful keys that will help you persevere. However, you must have a made up mind to get up and continue the journey.

In an article written by Joyce Meyer, one of the world's leading practical Bible Teachers, she gave profound words of wisdom of the importance of having a made up mind.

I've Got My Mind Made Up!
By Joyce Meyer
http://www.joycemeyer.org/OurMinistries/EverydayAnswers/Articles/art26.htm

What condition is your mind in? Have you noticed its condition changes? One time you may be calm, peaceful and certain of yourself. Another time you're anxious, worried and insecure. There've been times in my own life when I've experienced these things. Sometimes I was able to easily make a decision and stick with it. Other times I couldn't seem to arrive at a decision at all. Doubt, fear and uncertainty haunted me mercilessly. I second-guessed myself and couldn't make up my mind.

I didn't know that I could do anything about my thought life. I thought I was destined to be indecisive. I believed in God—and had for many years—but I had no teaching at all about my thought life or the proper condition of a believer's mind. Years ago when I began to get a lot more serious about my relationship with the Lord, I learned that many of my problems with indecision were rooted in wrong thinking patterns. My mind was undisciplined. It was a mess! I doubt that it was ever in the condition it should've been, and if it was, it didn't last long. I felt overwhelmed when I began to see how indecisive and insecure I was. I tried hard to correct the problem by rejecting the wrong thoughts that came into my mind, but they were persistent.

Many people struggle with this because they have spent years allowing their minds to wander. They've never applied the principles of discipline to their thought lives. People who can't seem to concentrate long enough to make a decision think there is something wrong with their mind. However, the inability to concentrate and make a decision can be the result of years of simply letting the mind do whatever it wants to do.

I struggled with this lack of ability to concentrate for years. When a strong decision was called for in my life, I found that I wasn't confident or disciplined enough to step out and make that choice. My mind was undisciplined and wandered from the subject at hand. I had to train my mind through discipline. It wasn't easy, and sometimes I still have relapses. While trying to complete a project, I'll suddenly realize that my mind has just wandered onto something else that has absolutely nothing to do with the issue at hand. I have not yet arrived at a place of perfect concentration, but at least I understand how important it is not to allow my mind to go wherever it wishes, whenever it desires.

Many times your mind can wander, even during conversation. There are times when someone may be talking to me and I listen for a while; then all of a sudden, I realize that I haven't heard a thing the person may have said. Why? Because I allowed my mind to wander onto something else. My body was standing there appearing to listen, but in my mind I didn't hear a thing.

For many years, when this sort of thing happened, I pretended that I knew exactly what Dave was saying. Now I simply stop and say, "Can you back up and repeat that? I let my mind wander, and I didn't hear a thing you said." In this way, I'm dealing with the problem. I'm disciplining my mind to stay on track. Confronting these issues is the only way to get on the victorious side of them.

Remember, the mind is the battlefield for these daily battles. Indecision and uncertainty are just results of losing these battles, and they can cause you to think there's something wrong with your mind. But the truth is your mind just needs to be disciplined. Ask God to help you, and then refuse to allow your mind to think about whatever it pleases. Begin today to control your thoughts and keep your mind on what you're doing. You'll need to practice for a while; breaking old habits and forming new ones always takes time. Discipline is never easy, but it's always worth it in the end. When you win the battle for your mind, you'll be much more certain of yourself, and you'll be able to make up your mind with confidence.

- - -

When you weigh out all options of "why" you need to do anything, your view of "how" you will do something will be out-weighed. After you make your mind up to do something, you will learn the importance to never get caught up on how, simply because your strength will rely solely on strong inner thought processes, that will allow you to automatically connect the dots, and put pieces together perfectly.

DESIRE

Something wished for. . .

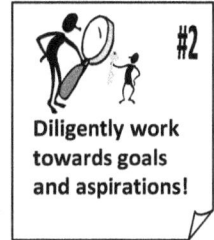

Diligently work towards goals and aspirations!

#2

"Whatsoever thy hand findeth to do, do it with thy might; for there is no work, nor device, nor knowledge, nor wisdom, in the grave, whither thou goest."
– Ecc 9:10 KJV

Let's begin by recognizing the power of desire. When we ignite desire in the inner sanctum of our being (which is in fact a chamber in our mind), we are ultimately choosing to think about something we actually want to be fulfilled. Thoughts have the ability to be put into action, therefore when you think a thing don't be afraid of what the outcome will be. You must be bold enough to recognize that you and you alone have the power to harvest the fruit of your thoughts that can and will create a lasting impression.

Whatever decisions you make, believe that desire is the initial core element to how your foundation will be laid and then will determine how you build up from there. Through desire, an individual can stand on faith to believe something wished for will come to fruition. If you choose not to desire better, then most times you will simply settle for just good, which is taking a mindset of accepting what life throws at you. You must learn to establish an outlook on the direction of how you want to live out your life. Consequently, you have the power to clearly layout blueprints and take control of your destiny.

People often try to look for easier ways to do things; they will cut corners in everything that they do, simply because they don't want to work hard for what they desire to gain out of life. Many times we think we want to climb to the mountain top, but hardly take the time to research the process it would take to go the extreme distance. Attempting to take the easy way out in everything will cause a person to miss out on opportunities of success. Indeed, it is better to work hard, strategize a plan of action, so that you can reap a lasting reward for your labor sown.

DREAM

Something hoped for. . .

Visualize a successful ending from the beginning. #3

Taking the First Step . . .

Success is a process, people can dream of it, believe for it, but may lack an understanding of what it will take to achieve it or the time it will take to obtain it. The steps to success before a person will reach their desired outcome may be as simple as lifting one foot up, and continuing to move upward. You have chosen to take the first step by making a decision to reboot your life, now reality of abundant success is actually only a few steps higher, and the sky is the limit.

When you have the ambition to anticipate something coming to fruition, you gain an instinct ability to desire pushing beyond all obstacles that may stand in your way. However, the persistence toward surpassing difficult to obtain or out of reach places must start within the dreamer in order to emphatically cause the dream to come alive.

Everyone should have dreams and establish personal goals for continued growth. I have learned a very important lesson in life about dreaming: A dream will only die, if the dreamer stops dreaming. It is extremely important to visualize your dreams coming to pass. If you work hard in hopes to see your dreams manifest, build firm foundations, write plans, set expectations, persevere beyond shortcomings, and take action to achieve them, you will make it to the top of the success ladder and reach unlimited possibilities.

EVALUATION BLUEPRINTS: DAY 1 - 7

Prepare your 7-day Life Blueprints!

Before beginning your 90-Day "Life Reboot" you will need to evaluate present daily life habits. Just as if you were starting a new diet, the decisions you make mentally on how you should prepare for the diet will be imperative as to how you will maintain the diet. On the following pages take time to blueprint daily life tasks, be sure to put into perspective life events and document what your daily regime consists of each day for no less than 7-days.

Day 1 - Blueprints

Date: _____

Day: _____

Morning Starting Time: _____

_____

_____

Mid-Morning Time/Event(s): _____

_____

_____

_____

Afternoon Time/Event(s): _____

_____

_____

_____

Mid-Day Event(s): _____

_____

_____

Evening Time/Event(s): _____

_____

_____

_____

_____

_____

_____

Day 2 - Blueprints

Date: _____

Day: _____

Morning Starting Time: _____

_____

_____

Mid-Morning Time/Event(s): _____

_____

_____

_____

Afternoon Time/Event(s): _____

_____

_____

_____

Mid-Day Event(s): _____

_____

_____

Evening Time/Event(s): _____

_____

_____

_____

_____

_____

_____

_____

Day 3 - Blueprints

Date: _____

Day: _____

Morning Starting Time: _____

_____

_____

Mid-Morning Time/Event(s): _____

_____

_____

_____

Afternoon Time/Event(s): _____

_____

_____

_____

Mid-Day Event(s): _____

_____

_____

Evening Time/Event(s): _____

_____

_____

_____

_____

_____

_____

_____

Day 4 - Blueprints

Date: _____

Day: _____

_____

_____

Mid-Morning Time/Event(s): _____

_____

_____

_____

Afternoon Time/Event(s): _____

_____

_____

_____

Mid-Day Event(s): _____

_____

_____

Evening Time/Event(s): _____

_____

_____

_____

_____

_____

_____

_____

Day 5 - Blueprints

Date: _____

Day: _____

Morning Starting Time: _____

_____

_____

Mid-Morning Time/Event(s): _____

_____

_____

_____

Afternoon Time/Event(s): _____

_____

_____

_____

Mid-Day Event(s): _____

_____

_____

Evening Time/Event(s): _____

_____

_____

_____

_____

_____

_____

_____

Day 6 - Blueprints

Date: _____

Day: _____

Morning Starting Time: _____

_____

_____

Mid-Morning Time/Event(s): _____

_____

_____

_____

Afternoon Time/Event(s): _____

_____

_____

_____

Mid-Day Event(s): _____

_____

_____

Evening Time/Event(s): _____

_____

_____

_____

_____

_____

_____

_____

Day 7 - Blueprints

Date: _____

Day: _____

Morning Starting Time: _____

_____

_____

Mid-Morning Time/Event(s): _____

_____

_____

_____

Afternoon Time/Event(s): _____

_____

_____

_____

Mid-Day Event(s): _____

_____

_____

Evening Time/Event(s): _____

_____

_____

_____

_____

_____

_____

_____

Studies have shown that every human being handle multiple areas pertaining to their total well being throughout their life that should have great importance. However the degree of importance will differentiate. In particular, "Making the Decision to find balance in your life" focuses on six core areas consisting of spiritual growth, financial stability, physical health, social interaction, goal and career planning, and time management.

Before continuing onto the 'Altering' stage it is important to be honest and clear about what the past week has shown you regarding habits you essentially formulated that may have caused a lack of control, stagnation and/or imbalance in your life currently. In the 'Alter' segment beginning on page 42 you will be introduced to six-core life areas that will help you organize and create a defined plan of action. After you have disciplined yourself in the six core areas, you will then need to take time to analyze and pin-point areas of habit. These specific areas may indeed have proven to be areas of hindrance and/or procrastination from allowing you to breakthrough a "stuck" mentality.

– – –

ALT(ER)

Alterations you decide to make in your life today,
will determine the destiny for your tomorrow...

Day: 8~77

ALTER

Alter means having the ability to make changes to something or somebody.

- ***Vary:*** *become different in some particular way, without permanently losing one's self or former characteristics or essence, either partially or wholly.*
- ***Modify***

The hard part is complete; blueprinting life events is a great big step towards making a decision to harness change of direction. Blueprints you constructed of your daily life endeavors over the last couple of days gave you an opportunity to decide on areas of your life that you must take better control over.

Taking time to discover areas of life concerns that eventually have become unproductive, should open up a window of opportunity for an individual to construct a plan that will outline promising alterations. When we choose to alter something, we have come to the conclusion that what once worked is no longer moving along as smoothly as we initially had hoped.

Daily life choices you engage in on a regular basis that you are not completely satisfied with may require you to implement alterations in your way of thinking as to how you determine choices initially. Over the next couple of weeks you will learn how to organize decisions you should make in order to create stronger balance in your life. You will also learn how to think about: "what you think about" before you decide on a rational choice.

What do I mean by the statement: "you will learn how to think about what you think about?" Your actual thoughts are extremely powerful . . . everything that "Is" was first a thought. Anything that we do is based on a desired will, which in fact is a thought first, conceived in your mind. You can speak what you're thinking or do exactly what you think based on what the thought may be.

Understanding how powerful your thoughts are should cause you to realize that every one of your actions has the potential to produce good or bad results. In order to create balance and stability in how you allow your thoughts to develop into actions, you must use wisdom in your approach concerning every given situation.

TIME FOR ALTERATIONS

What areas in your life can you alter?

_____
_____
_____
_____
_____
_____
_____
_____

What areas of your life do you know are non-negotiable for altering?

_____
_____
_____
_____
_____
_____
_____
_____

What areas of your life can you better manage if you made certain alterations?

_____
_____
_____
_____
_____
_____
_____
_____

ORGANIZE: DAY 8 - 12

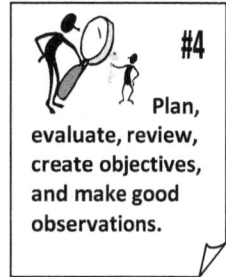

#4 Plan, evaluate, review, create objectives, and make good observations.

Organization is creating a balance or finding equilibrium between multiple variables. In order to define areas of your life that honestly should be in order you will need to first tackle the assignment of taking inventory of current life cluttered areas. Clutter can derive from starting and stopping task you set out to do. You may have an unfinished project that has been left sitting or idle for some time, weather de-junking a closet to even writing that novel you have always desired to finish.

When you lose momentum from accomplishing any goal you set out to do, you are ultimately creating a cluttered pessimistic environment around you. Unfinished business or things in your way can hold you back and cause you to be stagnant from moving forward with goals and dreams. When things are out of place, you can acquire unintentional tiredness, simply brought on because you have allowed time, space, things to obscure your view.

Begin to look around you: home, work, school, family, social interactions, time management, reflection-time, finances, goals and aspirations. Based on your 7-day blueprints you prepared, find out where you can begin to inventory the areas you spent less time or wasted time or lacked momentum in completion, and figure out where you can create a more productive perspective. Search deep into those areas that have literally stayed dormant for years that are unfinished, decide if you should simply discard the idea, or strategize a plan where you can map out a specific course of action.

Key Points:
- If you cannot finish a task within a reasonable amount of time, be sure to place everything in an order that you know you can easily go right back to with a plan of completion.

- Create short-time frames when working on task; put all ideas into an isolated visual viewpoint.

- Write down objectives as to how you foresee accomplishing projects you set out to do.

SIX CORE AREAS: DAY 9

We have so many different parts to our lives, family and friends, career, health, personal and spiritual growth, managing life goals, just to name a few. Nonetheless, having the ability to de-clutter and maintain balance in all core areas can be a challenge, but it is doable.

#5

Master the six core areas of total well being.

When we begin to give more attention to one area more than the other, that is when our life can get chaotic so to speak. Depending upon our focus at any given point in our lives, if we don't pay close attention to pressing issues, we may forget or tend to not give much thought to other areas that may in fact need the most concentration.

Today however, is the day to start looking at imbalanced areas in our life in order to create equilibrium. Following is a coaching tool called a "life wheel," we will use it to obtain clarity into the areas that might be out of balance.

Based on the six core areas that will be introduced on the following life wheel, using a scale from 1–10, where 1=unhappy and 10=completely satisfied, *how would you rate the balance in your life?*

THE LIFE WHEEL

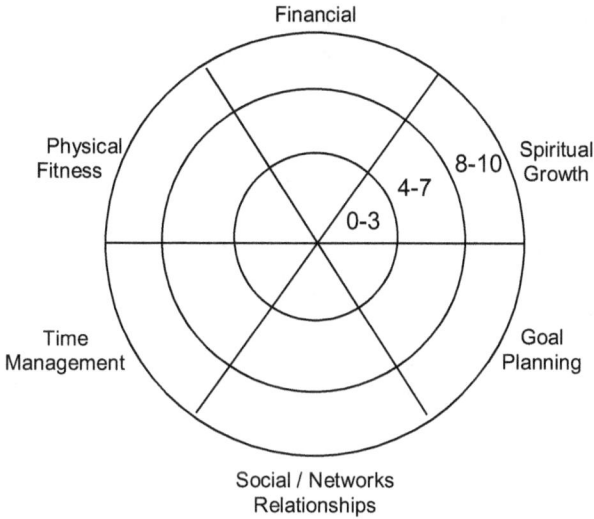

After you give each area a score, shade in the assigned number, to see where your "wheel" is unaligned. Is your wheel round and able to roll, or do you have a flat somewhere?

Where your wheel is not round is an indication of which areas of your life you will need the most attention. **The goal is to bring all areas to about the same level of balance "10",** within the next 82 days you will be able to journal how you make daily life decisions in each core area.

A "10" in every area would be ideal, but even an "8" would be okay. You will discover as you begin to level out your life wheel, even if the level is still not where you desire it to be, you will begin to feel as though you have a lot more control in your life.

SIX CORE AREA(S) OF FOCUS: DAY 10

Looking at the illustration of the six evolving core areas, what is your <u>central area of focus</u>? Write over the light colored area what your central core area is.

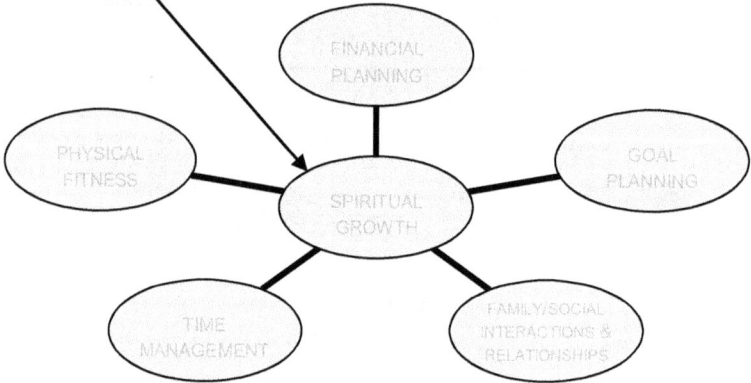

Based on importance to you, prioritize the six core areas:

1. **Spiritual Growth:** Daily Prayer & Study Time, Self-Reflection
2. **Financial Strategies:** Budget Planning, Checks & Balances, Savings Plan, Investments
3. **Physical Fitness:** Healthy Eating Habits, Maintain Good Daily Workout Plan
4. **Social Interactions:** Time Spent with Family, Friends, Social Events, Relationships
5. **Goal Planning:** Career Plans, Vision, Educational Pursuit
6. **Time Management:** Schedule of Daily, Weekly, Annual Tasks

1. _____ : _____

2. _____ : _____

3. _____ : _____

4. _____ : _____

5. _____ : _____

6. _____ : _____

What Is At Your Core? : DAY 11 - 12

Depending upon what the core area of your life is will ultimately determine where balance derives from in your life. As you are working on your life wheel alignment, you will begin to realize that whatever you believe to be the most valuable priority to you, all areas will stem out of that, but the core will have the greatest weight.

Within the next couple of pages you will be given strategies that will help you realize core values in order to create balance. You will learn how to level-out your life wheel, and areas of your life will begin to evolve around what you believe to be a priority in your life.

When you identify priorities and what you value most, it will be easy for you to stop what is not working, and pursue what does work. Balancing your life in order to create change of direction will no longer seem like a chore. You will recognize how to connect the dots effortlessly.

The following is an example of how to pin-point areas of imbalance:

What is not working: "*I keep coming up short every month on my bills.*" You are finding that you go to work every day, you have less momentum to share fun outings with family, and you seem to be a little more edgy with others.

Determine how it got that way: Maybe you have not really established a budget and have adopted the "Rob Peter to Pay Paul" mentality. Or, you may just feel that you need to continuously apply for more credit, in order to pay off old debts. Then you actually sink deeper into more debt, causing you to feel guilty and stuck with no idea on who to turn to for help. Then you decide not to spend time with others, because it simply just depends on what your check will look like each pay.

How to fix it? A simple route to take will be to purchase a spiral notebook, and specifically use it as a budget notebook; write down monies you obtain, and all expenditures you have. Or, you can order a budget planner at: http://www.appleseedpd.com/Publications.html to use as a guide to also help you master easy financial strategies.

Now take steps towards balancing all six core life areas, begin by documenting what is not working, determine how the situation got that way, and work on fixing it using the following balancing table.

Balancing Table: Taking steps towards balance

CORE AREA	Figure out what is not working	Determine how it got that way	Work on how to fix it
Spiritual Growth			
Financial Planning			
Health & Fitness			
Social Interactions			
Time Management			
Goal Planning			

CREATE AN ACTION PLAN: DAY 13 - 77

After completing your evaluation and you have decided what is not working and determined how it got that way, now it is time to create a plan of action. Discover what decisions you will need to make to formulate balance. The first time you create your action plan, you're going to spend a couple of weeks mastering how to determine the best outcome when making decisions. This is the upfront cost of organizing your life. However, once you've done it, you'll be amazed at how much more in control you will feel.

#6
Create a consistent checks & balance system for everyday life matters.

The following are specific steps to help guide you on drafting your action plan.

Step #1
After you have identified areas of imbalance, decide exactly what the biggest problem areas are that should be re-balanced. Why should these areas be re-balanced? You can do this by mapping out a 24-hour daily time schedule on the following page.

Step #2
Categorize information. Based on the six-core areas, what factors create problems, time restraints and limitations to pursuing better manageable resolutions?

Step #3
Make observations in order to identify possible alternatives.

Step #4
Brainstorm and generate daily logs and journals to discover ideas for possible solutions. You can begin to initiate this process within the following pages, over the next couple of weeks.

Step #5
Create a daily checks and balance system to evaluate each choice in terms of its consequences. A wise master builder always counts up the cost to any decision made towards structuring something being built-up. Use your standards and personal judgment to determine the pros and cons of each alternative solution you choose each day.

Step #6

Determine the best alternative. This is much easier after you have structured a decision-making mapping process for a couple of weeks.

Step #7

After a couple of weeks of observations and evaluation use a couple of days to document changes you noticed or patterns you discovered in the digest journal on page 109.

Step #8

Evaluate the outcome of your decisions and begin to create action steps towards pin-pointing areas of hindrance. This is an important step for further development of your decision making skills and judgment. You will begin this process during the 'Delete' segment of your readings.

DECISION-MAKING MAPPING PROCESS

Once you have utilized mapping tools within "Making the Decision: Alter(ing)" section, you may desire to create a similar process / action program on your own to use on a continual basis. You can purchase a goal planner, to document daily life endeavors and longer term goals at: http://www.appleseedpd.com/Publications.html.

Map out what your daily schedule looks like, and how much time you allow for each area.

Day One
Week Day: _____ What time does your day began?
_____

Example:
4:45 a.m. – Prayer Time
(Spiritual Enrichment)
5:45 a.m. – Exercise (Physical
Fitness), (Personal Time)
6:30 a.m. – Refresh (Personal
Time)
7 a.m. – Breakfast (Health)
7:30 a.m. – Commute &
Reflection Time (Time)
8 a.m. – Begin Work Day
(Financial Planning)
12 p.m. – Lunch Time (Health)
1 p.m. – Reflection Time (Goal Planning)

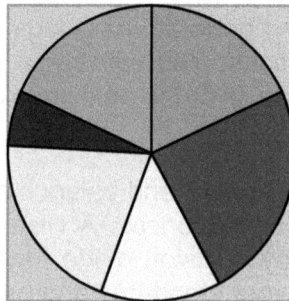

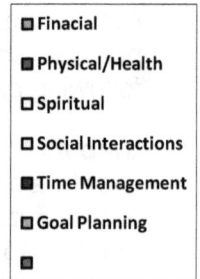

- ▣ Finacial
- ■ Physical/Health
- ☐ Spiritual
- ☐ Social Interactions
- ■ Time Management
- ▣ Goal Planning
- ▣

2 p.m. – Work (Financial Planning)
4:30 p.m. – Daily Wrap-up & Commute (Time)
5:30 p.m. – Dinner (Health) - Family Time (Social)
6:30 p.m. – Reflection Focus (Goal Planning)
7 p.m. – Meetings (Financial), (Goal Planning), (Social)
8:30 p.m. – Next Day Prep (Personal / Family Time)
9:30 p.m. – Study Time (Goal Planning) (Spiritual Enrichment)
10 p.m. – Rest Time (Physical / Health)
4:45 a.m. – Begin a New Day w/ Prayer (Spiritual)

Document your daily schedule below, based on a 24 hr period:

_____ : _____ Time Allotted: _____

_____ : _____ Time Allotted: _____

_____ : _____ Time Allotted: _____

_____ : _____ Time Allotted: _____

_____ : _____ Time Allotted: _____

_____ : _____ Time Allotted: _____

_____ : _____ Time Allotted: _____

_____ : _____ Time Allotted: _____

_____ : _____ Time Allotted: _____

_____ : _____ Time Allotted: _____

_____ : _____ Time Allotted: _____

_____ : _____ Time Allotted: _____

_____ : _____ Time Allotted: _____

_____ : _____ Time Allotted: _____

_____ : _____ Time Allotted: _____

_____ : _____ Time Allotted: _____

_____ : _____ Time Allotted: _____

_____ : _____ Time Allotted: _____

_____ : _____ Time Allotted: _____

_____ : _____ Time Allotted: _____

_____ : _____ Time Allotted: _____

_____ : _____ Time Allotted: _____

_____ : _____ Time Allotted: _____

Based on the time you allow for each core area in your life, in order to get a good picture of where your life might be out of balance, tally up your time for each category within a 7-day period:

Example table:

Core Area	Mon.	Tues	Wed.	Thurs.	Friday	Sat.	Sun.	Total
Spiritual Growth	2	4	2	2	2	3	6	20
Financial Planning	9	7	9	8	9		2	42
Physical Fitness	8	6	8	7	6	6	5	45
Social Interaction		3		2	4	7	3	22
Time Mgt.	3	2	3	4	2	4	3	23
Goal Planning	2	2	2	1	1	4	5	16
Total Hrs.	24	24	24	24	24	24	24	168

Create your own table:

Core Area	Mon.	Tues.	Wed.	Thurs.	Friday	Sat.	Sun.	Total
Spiritual Growth								
Financial Planning								
Physical Fitness								
Social Interaction								
Time Mgt.								
Goal Planning								
Total Hrs.								

Tally up your score:

	Spiritual Growth	Financial	Physical / Fitness	Social	Time Mgt.	Goal Planning
i.e.	20 hrs	42 hrs	45 hrs	22 hrs	23 hrs	16 hrs
Time Allotted						

Now that you have tallied up your scores, began to use the next couple of weeks to journal daily observations. Each week should show an improved strategy to making wiser decisions towards creating a balance in core areas that have long seemed impossible to manage.

Creating Structure

The purpose of becoming acclimated to the six-core principles over the next couple of weeks is to assist you with structure. As you layout a daily planned regime you will in actuality be constructing a pathway towards finding total and complete balance.

Structure will help you put life concerns into a more focused perspective. When you lack structure or imbalance in one area, nine-times out of ten you will find that other areas of your life will be unaligned as well.

As you learn how to incorporate daily structure in your life given through the six-core areas, you will begin to develop a fervent prayer life, which is imperative before handling any decisions. You will become better equipped to handle your finances, health, goals and how to effectively manage your time. Striving towards creating structure in whatever task you desire to take on each day will allow you to obtain the greatest level of optimum results and confidence in making wise decisions.

Be diligent in working on all six-core areas each day.

Go for it!

SPIRITUAL GROWTH

"Even though millions of prayers are rendered by millions of people every minute of every day, there is something about having enough faith to believe, that regardless of that truth, your prayers will be heard and answered." – *J. M. Newby*

Prayer is communication with God, and a key element to accessing answers, instructions and directions as to how your daily steps should be taken. Anyone can take on distressful thinking based on presenting circumstances, sudden and/or unexpected life events that occur. However, when you ponder upon things that you do not have the power to change or control versus areas of life that you can control, you will inadvertently place yourself in a posture of indecision.

Create impressionable blueprints, as you pave out footprints through your journey of life.

As a result you can then seem to become stuck in a position of complacency. Understand, life will continue regardless of daily time spent on contemplating a matter you need to make a decision on. Nevertheless, you have power to alter your thinking and outcome if you believe by faith that all things will work together for your good either way. Establishing a fervent prayer life will give you power to confidently move forward on decisions you make with momentum. You will begin to place God in charge of your decision making process with an expectancy that results you obtain will always far exceed any regrets you may acquire.

Reaching this level of confidence will cause spiritual growth. Your prayer life will be an outward demonstration of your faith an acknowledgment of your desire to trust God's direction an initiate the process of resolution for any and every situation. Allowing God to orchestrate and direct your life path is ultimately choosing to live a successful abundant life.

I recall a great preacher emphatically proving this statement when he shared an absolute profound definition to unlocking success for one's life. He proclaimed that "success is complete obedience to God." This

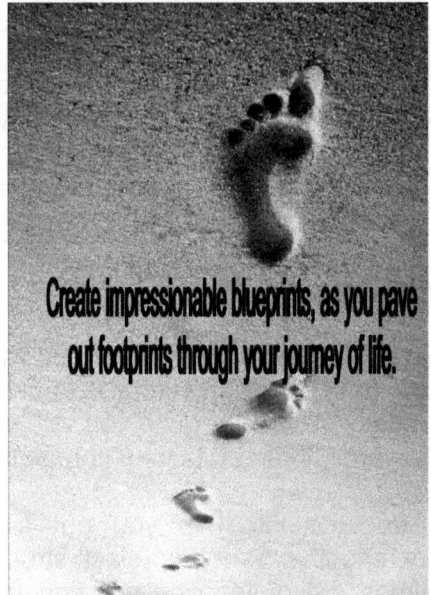

statement being understood would then signify that the purpose and perfect plan specifically ordained for every individual life is already predestined. As a matter of fact, an individual does not necessarily need to try to figure most things out. Prayer, belief and walking in faith, obeying God's instruction will allow access to answers that were never intended for one to work hard to obtain.

Over the next couple of weeks, take the opportunity to set aside an appointed time daily to pray and study the word. Document your prayer request and answers you obtain during your time spent in communication with God. Each day you should see an increase in your time spent in prayer. You will discover a foundation built up by faith that will be immovable.

A recognizable prayer you can start off with or follow is the Lord's Prayer:

[9] Our Father which art in heaven, Hallowed be thy name.
[10] Thy kingdom come, Thy will be done in earth, as it is in heaven.
[11] Give us this day our daily bread.
[12] And forgive us our debts, as we forgive our debtors.
[13] And lead us not into temptation, but deliver us from evil:
For thine is the kingdom, and the power, and the glory, forever.
Amen. – *Matthew 6:9-13 KJV*

DAILY MEDITATION / REFLECTION

Build spiritual growth by setting aside an appointed time daily to pray and study the word.

WEEK 1: *DAY 14 - 20*

DAY 1 – Date: Time Spent: _____

_____

_____

DAY 2 – Date: Time Spent: _____

_____

_____

DAY 3 – Date: Time Spent: _____

_____

_____

DAY 4 – Date: Time Spent: _____

_____

_____

DAY 5 – Date: Time Spent: _____

_____

_____

DAY 6 – Date: Time Spent: _____

_____

_____

DAY 7 – Date: Time Spent: _____

_____

Weekly Meditation Scripture: "But seek ye first the kingdom of God, and his righteousness; and all these things shall be added unto you." – Matthew 6:33 KJV

Write your own weekly word(s) of declaration:

_____

_____

DAILY MEDITATION / REFLECTION

Set aside an appointed time daily to pray and study the word.

WEEK 2: *DAY 21 - 27*

DAY 1 – Date: Time Spent: _____

_____

_____

DAY 2 – Date: Time Spent: _____

_____

_____

DAY 3 – Date: Time Spent: _____

_____

_____

DAY 4 – Date: Time Spent: _____

_____

_____

DAY 5 – Date: Time Spent: _____

_____

_____

DAY 6 – Date: Time Spent: _____

_____

_____

DAY 7 – Date: Time Spent: _____

_____

_____

Weekly Meditation Scripture: The Prayer of Jabez: "And Jabez was more honourable than his brethren: and his mother called his name Jabez, saying, Because I bare him with sorrow. And Jabez called on the God of Israel, saying, Oh that thou wouldest bless me indeed, and enlarge my coast, and that thine hand might be with me, and that thou wouldest keep me from evil, that it may not grieve me! And God granted him that which he requested." *– 1 Chronicles 4:9-10 KJV*

Write your own weekly word(s) of declaration: _____

_____

DAILY MEDITATION / REFLECTION

Set aside an appointed time daily to pray and study the word.

WEEK 3: *DAY 28 - 34*

DAY 1 – Date: Time Spent: _____

_____

_____

DAY 2 – Date: Time Spent: _____

_____

_____

DAY 3 – Date: Time Spent: _____

_____

_____

DAY 4 – Date: Time Spent: _____

_____

_____

DAY 5 – Date: Time Spent: _____

_____

_____

DAY 6 – Date: Time Spent: _____

_____

_____

DAY 7 – Date: Time Spent: _____

_____

_____

Weekly Meditation Scripture: "Trust in the LORD with all thine heart; and lean not unto thine own understanding. In all thy ways acknowledge him, and he shall direct thy paths." – Proverbs 3:5-6 KJV

Write your own weekly word(s) of declaration:

_____

_____

DAILY MEDITATION / REFLECTION

Set aside an appointed time daily to pray and study the word.

WEEK 4: DAY 35 - 41

DAY 1 – Date: Time Spent: _____

_____

_____

DAY 2 – Date: Time Spent: _____

_____

_____

DAY 3 – Date: Time Spent: _____

_____

_____

DAY 4 – Date: Time Spent: _____

_____

_____

DAY 5 – Date: Time Spent: _____

_____

_____

DAY 6 – Date: Time Spent: _____

_____

_____

DAY 7 – Date: Time Spent: _____

_____

_____

Weekly Meditation Scripture: "If thou canst believe, all things are possible to him that believeth." – *Mark 9:23 KJV*

Write your own weekly word(s) of declaration: _____

_____

_____

DAILY MEDITATION / REFLECTION

Set aside an appointed time daily to pray and study the word.

WEEK 5: *DAY 42 - 48*

DAY 1 – Date: _____   Time Spent: _____

_____

_____

DAY 2 – Date: _____   Time Spent: _____

_____

_____

DAY 3 – Date: _____   Time Spent: _____

_____

_____

DAY 4 – Date: _____   Time Spent: _____

_____

_____

DAY 5 – Date: _____   Time Spent: _____

_____

_____

DAY 6 – Date: _____   Time Spent: _____

_____

_____

DAY 7 – Date: _____   Time Spent: _____

_____

_____

Weekly Meditation Scripture: "And this is the confidence that we have in him, that, if we ask any thing according to his will, he heareth us: And if we know that he hear us, whatsoever we ask, we know that we have the petitions that we desired of him."
– I John 5:14-15 KJV

Write your own weekly word(s) of declaration:

_____

_____

DAILY MEDITATION / REFLECTION

Set aside an appointed time daily to pray and study the word.

WEEK 6: DAY 49 - 55

DAY 1 – Date: Time Spent: _____

_____

_____

DAY 2 – Date: Time Spent: _____

_____

_____

DAY 3 – Date: Time Spent: _____

_____

_____

DAY 4 – Date: Time Spent: _____

_____

_____

DAY 5 – Date: Time Spent: _____

_____

_____

DAY 6 – Date: Time Spent: _____

_____

_____

DAY 7 – Date: Time Spent: _____

_____

_____

Weekly Meditation Scripture: "And we know that all things work together for good to them that love God, to them who are the called according to his purpose." – *Romans 8:28 KJV*

Write your own weekly word(s) of declaration: _____

_____

_____

DAILY MEDITATION / REFLECTION

Set aside an appointed time daily to pray and study the word.

WEEK 7: DAY 56 - 62

DAY 1 – Date: _____   Time Spent: _____

_____

_____

DAY 2 – Date: _____   Time Spent: _____

_____

_____

DAY 3 – Date: _____   Time Spent: _____

_____

_____

DAY 4 – Date: _____   Time Spent: _____

_____

_____

DAY 5 – Date: _____   Time Spent: _____

_____

_____

DAY 6 – Date: _____   Time Spent: _____

_____

_____

DAY 7 – Date: _____   Time Spent: _____

_____

_____

Weekly Meditation Scripture: "But my God shall supply all your need according to his riches in glory by Christ Jesus." – *Philippians 4:19 KJV*

Write your own weekly word(s) of declaration: _____

_____

_____

DAILY MEDITATION / REFLECTION

Set aside an appointed time daily to pray and study the word.

WEEK 8: *DAY 63 - 69*

DAY 1 – Date: _____ Time Spent: _____

_____

_____

DAY 2 – Date: _____ Time Spent: _____

_____

_____

DAY 3 – Date: _____ Time Spent: _____

_____

_____

DAY 4 – Date: _____ Time Spent: _____

_____

_____

DAY 5 – Date: _____ Time Spent: _____

_____

_____

DAY 6 – Date: _____ Time Spent: _____

_____

_____

DAY 7 – Date: _____ Time Spent: _____

_____

_____

Weekly Meditation Scripture: "I can do all things through Christ which strengtheneth me." *– Philippians 4:13 KJV*

Write your own weekly word(s) of declaration: _____

_____

_____

PROPER DIET & PHYSICAL FITNESS

What actually defines a healthy lifestyle? Scientific evidence has reinforced the impression that regular exercise, and nutrition combined are two major components to a healthy lifestyle. Exercise and regular physical activity, and nutritional eating benefit the body, a sedentary lifestyle does the opposite (D. Bender & B. Leon, 1996, p. 55).

Making the decision to reboot a sedentary lifestyle decreases the chances of becoming overweight and developing a number of chronic diseases. Additionally, regular physical activity and good eating habits will improve your chances of living longer and living healthier. Physically active adults in comparison to sedentary counterparts tend to develop and maintain higher levels of physical fitness. Within the United States it has been estimated that as many as 250,000 deaths occur per year, and approximately 12% of that total are attributed to a lack of regular physical activity (D. Bender & B. Leone, 1996, p. 57).

Early nutrition is essential to offset future chronic diseases. In building or maintaining a healthy lifestyle, understanding the importance of good nutrition is vital. Studies have increased to show the potential benefit of early nutrition involving children and young adults. Nutrition can be established through the four food group plan the foundation for a good diet. A practical approach to sound nutrition is to categorize food that make similar nutrient contribution and then provide servings from each category in the daily diet (F. Katch & W. McArdle, 1988, p. 42).

If you can develop a habit of creating daily menus based on the Four Food Group Plan and dietary exchange method developed by the American Dietetic Association you will be well on your way to better health. It is amazing even though the Basic Four food group is familiar to many adults, most people do not know how to use the simple system.

Categories of the foods in the four-food group plan consist of: milk, meat, vegetables and fruits, cereal and grains. More servings of grains and fruits and vegetables are recommended for optimal health. Dietitians and exercise specialists have applied computer technology in the formulation of well-balanced meals and exercise programs for weight control. However, if you focus more attention to the quality and quantity of a basic daily diet, along with promotion of healthy levels of physical activity to maintain a certain energy balance you will create longevity.

Adults of all ages should participate in some form of daily physical activity. Physical fitness is generally achieved through exercise, correct nutrition and enough rest. Physical fitness is considered a measure of the body's ability to function efficiently and effectively in work and leisure activities and to be healthy. Participation in regular physical activity— at least 30 minutes of moderate activity on at least five days per week, or 20 minutes of vigorous physical activity at least three times per week—is critical to sustaining good health.

Balance your overall physical fitness & health conscious thinking.

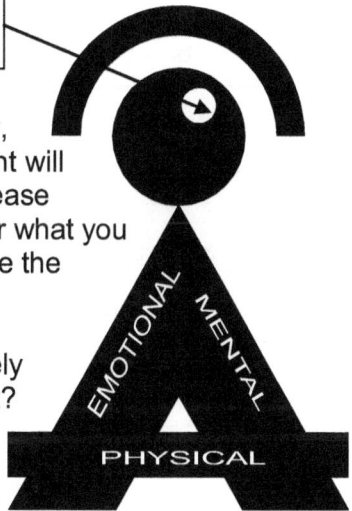

Learning to increase your physical activity, and incorporate a healthier eating regiment will decrease your vulnerability to chronic disease risk factors. Knowledge is power, however what you do with it or how you apply it will determine the actual strength.

Be honest with yourself, are you completely satisfied with your overall health or weight? If not decide what areas you are determined to work on, such as better eating habits, or maintaining consistency with a daily exercise regimen.

On the following pages, take time to create a daily food and physical fitness log, in order to create balance in this core area. Physical fitness and optimum health; it is an important part of life.

What is the main goal you desire to accomplish pertaining to physical fitness and optimum health?

DAILY FOOD & PHYSICAL FITNESS LOG

Document fitness goals *(be sure to take measurements)* and what you will eat daily for an entire week.

Week 1: Day 14 - 20	Beginning Weight:	Ending Weight:

Weekly Fitness Goals:

Date:		Day:		Time Spent:
Breakfast				
Lunch				
Dinner				
Exercise				
Measurements	Arms:	Legs:	Waist:	Hips:

Date:		Day:		Time Spent:
Breakfast				
Lunch				
Dinner				
Exercise				
Measurements	Arms:	Legs:	Waist:	Hips:

Date:		Day:		Time Spent:
Breakfast				
Lunch				
Dinner				
Exercise				
Measurements	Arms:	Legs:	Waist:	Hips:

Date:	Day:		Time Spent:	
Breakfast				
Lunch				
Dinner				
Exercise				
Measurements	Arms:	Legs:	Waist:	Hips:

Date:	Day:		Time Spent:	
Breakfast				
Lunch				
Dinner				
Exercise				
Measurements	Arms:	Legs:	Waist:	Hips:

Date:	Day:		Time Spent:	
Breakfast				
Lunch				
Dinner				
Exercise				
Measurements	Arms:	Legs:	Waist:	Hips:

Date:	Day:		Time Spent:	
Breakfast				
Lunch				
Dinner				
Exercise				
Measurements	Arms:	Legs:	Waist:	Hips:

DAILY FOOD & PHYSICAL FITNESS LOG

Document fitness goals *(be sure to take measurements)* and what you will eat daily for an entire week.

Week 2: *Day 21 – 27*	Beginning Weight:	Ending Weight:

Weekly Fitness Goals:		

Date: **Day:**   **Time Spent:**

Breakfast				
Lunch				
Dinner				
Exercise				
Measurements	Arms:	Legs:	Waist:	Hips:

Date: **Day:**   **Time Spent:**

Breakfast				
Lunch				
Dinner				
Exercise				
Measurements	Arms:	Legs:	Waist:	Hips:

Date: **Day:**   **Time Spent:**

Breakfast				
Lunch				
Dinner				
Exercise				
Measurements	Arms:	Legs:	Waist:	Hips:

Date: **Day:**   **Time Spent:**

Breakfast	
Lunch	
Dinner	
Exercise	
Measurements	Arms: Legs: Waist: Hips:

Date: **Day:**   **Time Spent:**

Breakfast	
Lunch	
Dinner	
Exercise	
Measurements	Arms: Legs: Waist: Hips:

Date: **Day:**   **Time Spent:**

Breakfast	
Lunch	
Dinner	
Exercise	
Measurements	Arms: Legs: Waist: Hips:

Date: **Day:**   **Time Spent:**

Breakfast	
Lunch	
Dinner	
Exercise	
Measurements	Arms: Legs: Waist: Hips:

DAILY FOOD & PHYSICAL FITNESS LOG

Document fitness goals *(be sure to take measurements)* and what you will eat daily for an entire week.

Week 3: Day 28 - 34	Beginning Weight:	Ending Weight:

Weekly Fitness Goals:

Date: Day: Time Spent:

Breakfast	
Lunch	
Dinner	
Exercise	
Measurements	Arms: Legs: Waist: Hips:

Date: Day: Time Spent:

Breakfast	
Lunch	
Dinner	
Exercise	
Measurements	Arms: Legs: Waist: Hips:

Date: Day: Time Spent:

Breakfast	
Lunch	
Dinner	
Exercise	
Measurements	Arms: Legs: Waist: Hips:

Date: **Day:**   **Time Spent:**

Breakfast				
Lunch				
Dinner				
Exercise				
Measurements	Arms:	Legs:	Waist:	Hips:

Date: **Day:**   **Time Spent:**

Breakfast				
Lunch				
Dinner				
Exercise				
Measurements	Arms:	Legs:	Waist:	Hips:

Date: **Day:**   **Time Spent:**

Breakfast				
Lunch				
Dinner				
Exercise				
Measurements	Arms:	Legs:	Waist:	Hips:

Date: **Day:**   **Time Spent:**

Breakfast				
Lunch				
Dinner				
Exercise				
Measurements	Arms:	Legs:	Waist:	Hips:

DAILY FOOD & PHYSICAL FITNESS LOG

Document fitness goals *(be sure to take measurements)* and what you will eat daily for an entire week.

Week 4: Day 35 - 41	Beginning Weight:	Ending Weight:
Weekly Fitness Goals:		

Date: **Day:**   **Time Spent:**

Breakfast	
Lunch	
Dinner	
Exercise	
Measurements	Arms: Legs: Waist: Hips:

Date: **Day:**   **Time Spent:**

Breakfast	
Lunch	
Dinner	
Exercise	
Measurements	Arms: Legs: Waist: Hips:

Date: **Day:**   **Time Spent:**

Breakfast	
Lunch	
Dinner	
Exercise	
Measurements	Arms: Legs: Waist: Hips:

Date:		Day:		Time Spent:	
Breakfast					
Lunch					
Dinner					
Exercise					
Measurements	**Arms:**	**Legs:**	**Waist:**	**Hips:**	

Date:		Day:		Time Spent:	
Breakfast					
Lunch					
Dinner					
Exercise					
Measurements	**Arms:**	**Legs:**	**Waist:**	**Hips:**	

Date:		Day:		Time Spent:	
Breakfast					
Lunch					
Dinner					
Exercise					
Measurements	**Arms:**	**Legs:**	**Waist:**	**Hips:**	

Date:		Day:		Time Spent:	
Breakfast					
Lunch					
Dinner					
Exercise					
Measurements	**Arms:**	**Legs:**	**Waist:**	**Hips:**	

DAILY FOOD & PHYSICAL FITNESS LOG

Document fitness goals *(be sure to take measurements)* and what you will eat daily for an entire week.

Week 5: Day 42 - 48	Beginning Weight:	Ending Weight:
Weekly Fitness Goals:		

Date: **Day:** **Time Spent:**

Breakfast	
Lunch	
Dinner	
Exercise	
Measurements	Arms: Legs: Waist: Hips:

Date: **Day:** **Time Spent:**

Breakfast	
Lunch	
Dinner	
Exercise	
Measurements	Arms: Legs: Waist: Hips:

Date: **Day:** **Time Spent:**

Breakfast	
Lunch	
Dinner	
Exercise	
Measurements	Arms: Legs: Waist: Hips:

Date: **Day:**   **Time Spent:**

Breakfast	
Lunch	
Dinner	
Exercise	
Measurements	Arms: Legs: Waist: Hips:

Date: **Day:**   **Time Spent:**

Breakfast	
Lunch	
Dinner	
Exercise	
Measurements	Arms: Legs: Waist: Hips:

Date: **Day:**   **Time Spent:**

Breakfast	
Lunch	
Dinner	
Exercise	
Measurements	Arms: Legs: Waist: Hips:

Date: **Day:**   **Time Spent:**

Breakfast	
Lunch	
Dinner	
Exercise	
Measurements	Arms: Legs: Waist: Hips:

DAILY FOOD & PHYSICAL FITNESS LOG

Document fitness goals *(be sure to take measurements)* and what you will eat daily for an entire week.

Week 6: *Day 49 - 55*	Beginning Weight:	Ending Weight:

Weekly Fitness Goals:

Date: **Day:**   **Time Spent:**

Breakfast	
Lunch	
Dinner	
Exercise	
Measurements	Arms: Legs: Waist: Hips:

Date: **Day:**   **Time Spent:**

Breakfast	
Lunch	
Dinner	
Exercise	
Measurements	Arms: Legs: Waist: Hips:

Date: **Day:**   **Time Spent:**

Breakfast	
Lunch	
Dinner	
Exercise	
Measurements	Arms: Legs: Waist: Hips:

Date:		Day:		Time Spent:	
Breakfast					
Lunch					
Dinner					
Exercise					
Measurements	Arms:	Legs:	Waist:	Hips:	

Date:		Day:		Time Spent:	
Breakfast					
Lunch					
Dinner					
Exercise					
Measurements	Arms:	Legs:	Waist:	Hips:	

Date:		Day:		Time Spent:	
Breakfast					
Lunch					
Dinner					
Exercise					
Measurements	Arms:	Legs:	Waist:	Hips:	

Date:		Day:		Time Spent:	
Breakfast					
Lunch					
Dinner					
Exercise					
Measurements	Arms:	Legs:	Waist:	Hips:	

DAILY FOOD & PHYSICAL FITNESS LOG

Document fitness goals *(be sure to take measurements)* and what you will eat daily for an entire week.

Week 7: Day 56 - 62	Beginning Weight:	Ending Weight:

Weekly Fitness Goals:

Date: **Day:** **Time Spent:**

Breakfast	
Lunch	
Dinner	
Exercise	
Measurements	Arms: Legs: Waist: Hips:

Date: **Day:** **Time Spent:**

Breakfast	
Lunch	
Dinner	
Exercise	
Measurements	Arms: Legs: Waist: Hips:

Date: **Day:** **Time Spent:**

Breakfast	
Lunch	
Dinner	
Exercise	
Measurements	Arms: Legs: Waist: Hips:

Date:		Day:		Time Spent:	
Breakfast					
Lunch					
Dinner					
Exercise					
Measurements	Arms:	Legs:	Waist:	Hips:	

Date:		Day:		Time Spent:	
Breakfast					
Lunch					
Dinner					
Exercise					
Measurements	Arms:	Legs:	Waist:	Hips:	

Date:		Day:		Time Spent:	
Breakfast					
Lunch					
Dinner					
Exercise					
Measurements	Arms:	Legs:	Waist:	Hips:	

Date:		Day:		Time Spent:	
Breakfast					
Lunch					
Dinner					
Exercise					
Measurements	Arms:	Legs:	Waist:	Hips:	

DAILY FOOD & PHYSICAL FITNESS LOG

Document fitness goals *(be sure to take measurements)* and what you will eat daily for an entire week.

Week 8: Day 63 - 69	Beginning Weight:	Ending Weight:

Weekly Fitness Goals:

Date:　　　　　　　　　　**Day:**　　　　　　**Time Spent:**

Breakfast	
Lunch	
Dinner	
Exercise	
Measurements	Arms:　　　Legs:　　　Waist:　　　Hips:

Date:　　　　　　　　　　**Day:**　　　　　　**Time Spent:**

Breakfast	
Lunch	
Dinner	
Exercise	
Measurements	Arms:　　　Legs:　　　Waist:　　　Hips:

Date:　　　　　　　　　　**Day:**　　　　　　**Time Spent:**

Breakfast	
Lunch	
Dinner	
Exercise	
Measurements	Arms:　　　Legs:　　　Waist:　　　Hips:

Date: Day: Time Spent:

Breakfast	
Lunch	
Dinner	
Exercise	
Measurements	Arms: Legs: Waist: Hips:

Date: Day: Time Spent:

Breakfast	
Lunch	
Dinner	
Exercise	
Measurements	Arms: Legs: Waist: Hips:

Date: Day: Time Spent:

Breakfast	
Lunch	
Dinner	
Exercise	
Measurements	Arms: Legs: Waist: Hips:

Date: Day: Time Spent:

Breakfast	
Lunch	
Dinner	
Exercise	
Measurements	Arms: Legs: Waist: Hips:

FINANCIAL MANAGEMENT

It's true – the rich get richer and the poor get poorer. Author Dave Ramsey suggests, "Money naturally flows from those who do not manage it to those who do." This raises an interesting question:

How can you make better decisions that will put you in the "rich get richer" category?

1. The first step is to establish a plan for managing resources you have. Utilize a spending plan (financial budget), you can purchase one at: http://www.appleseedpd.com/Publications.html. Without one, your money will disappear quickly, and you'll constantly be controlled by a "lack of money". Financial pressure will become a way of life.

2. Step two, cut out un-necessary spending. Creating a budget will cause you to pinpoint areas where you have been spending more than you realized. Often times, the problem is not having enough income; it is usually too much lifestyle. You may not be able to increase your income right away, but you can immediately take action by cutting expenses. You may have to stop buying fast food, downgrade to a less expensive car, and stay away from clearance sales. Be diligent and committed in controlling what is within your control.

3. Most important step: begin tithing immediately 10% of all your increase. Your increase is based on monies you obtain as an income for work and/or labor you perform. "Give, Give, Give," and once you master this skill "Give some more", and watch an increase in your current resources. If you do not take on a giving mentality, steps 1 and 2 above will work for a certain amount of time, but it will not necessarily place you in the "rich get richer" category, which is ultimate abundance.

Despite your best efforts, you will possibly continue to fall in the "poor get poorer" crowd if you lack courage in giving. If you wait until you can afford to tithe or take on a giving mentality, you never will. Fear of giving away what you believe you do not have to give, will cause you to not be open to receive above and beyond what you could have.

Mismanagement of your finances is an individual behavior and you will experience rewards and/or consequences. Properly manage the resources you have, performing the three steps given above will lay a good foundation for your financial success and position you to receive good rewards for your diligence. Take personal responsibility for your finances, make wise money management decisions, and more money will come your way.

Use the tools on the following pages to help you create a good start to making better financial management decisions.

FINANCIAL

Write out plans as to how you believe you can improve your financial status. What are major areas that need improvement, categorize them from 1 through 5.

1.

2.

3.

4.

5.

List areas that you spend either emotionally or socially:

Emotional Spending

_____

_____

Social Spending

_____

_____

What is your overall current net worth? _____

Decipher between your assets and liabilities.

Net Worth	Assets	Liabilities

Every day for the next 8-weeks, follow a plan of action that will allow you to realistically strategize how you can manage your financial matters.

CREATE A FINANCIAL ACTION PLAN

Strategize a plan of action as to how you can revamp your spending habits.

_____

_____

_____

Over the next 8-weeks establish a set savings goal you desire to achieve, be specific in how you plan to acquire, and save your desired goal amount.

During the month of: _____, I desire to focus on saving: $_____. I will accumulate this savings amount through focusing on the following steps:

_____

_____

_____

During the month of: _____, I desire to focus on saving: $_____. I will accumulate this savings amount through focusing on the following steps:

_____

_____

_____

During the month of: _____, I desire to focus on saving: $_____. I will accumulate this savings amount through focusing on the following steps:

_____

_____

_____

- Consider purchasing a budget planner, which you can carry along with you daily in order to organize all your financial matters. We recommend ordering a copy of: "The Pocket Financial Planner", you can obtain at: www.appleseedpd.com/Publications.html.

- Order a free annual credit report:
  https://annualcreditreport.transunion.com

- Contact them at: 1.866.478.0030 to dispute old debt accounts on your credit report.

  - **By Mail:**
    Trans Union Consumer Relations
    PO Box 2000
    Chester, PA 19022-2000

  - **By Phone:** 1-800-916-8800

  - If you need assistance with a kick-start to re-establishing good spending habits, or clearing up old debt accounts contact a credit counseling company at: 1.800.547.5005.

BUDGET: *MONTH 1 ~ DAY 14 - 41*

Over the next couple of weeks establish a monthly budget plan as follows:

Monthly Income Received			
Date	Categories *(Source of funds)*	Amount	

C – cash
D – debit
Chk – check
MO – money order

Categories	Amount Due	Amount Paid	Date	Form of Pmt. C/D/Chk/MO	Balance
TITHES /OFFERING					
MORTGAGE / RENT					
HOMEOWNERS INS.					
TAXES					
HOME MAINTENANCE					
GAS / ELECTRIC					
WATER					
GROCERIES					
TELEPHONE					
TRANSPORTATION					
AUTO INSURANCE					
GASOLINE					
LIFE INSURANCE					
HEALTH / DENTAL					
PRESCRIPTIONS					
CHILD / AFTER SCHOOL CARE					
EDUCATION EXP.					

Categories	Amount Due	Amount Paid	Date	Form of Pmt. C/D/Chk/MO	Balance
CABLE / INTERNET					
CLEANERS / LAUNDRY					
CLOTHING EXPENSE					
CREDIT CARD:					
CREDIT CARD:					
CREDIT CARD:					
MISC. EXPENSE:					
MISC. EXPENSE:					
MISC. EXPENSE:					
FAMILY HAIR CARE					
CELL PHONE:					
ENTERTAINMENT					
PUBLICATIONS / MAGAZINES					
SAVINGS / STOCK CONTRIBUTION					
TOTAL MONTHLY EXPENSES					

Record account reference and/or payment confirmation information and form of payment made:

Payment Categories	Account / Ref. / Confirmation #	Check #

Ending monthly balance: _____

DAILY EXPENDITURE: *WEEK 14 - 41*

Over the next couple of weeks establish a daily expenditure log:

Example

Date	Categories	Amount Paid	+ / -	Form of Pmt. C/D/Chk/MO	Balance
8/15	Groceries	210.00	-	D	17,500
	- Home, Work, Etc.				17,390

Date	Categories	Amount Paid	+ / -	Form of Pmt. C/D/Chk/MO	Balance
	ENDING MONTHLY BALANCE				

C – cash   *D – debit/credit*   *Chk – check*   *MO – money order*

BUDGET: MONTH 2 ~ DAY 42 - 69

Continue to follow the monthly budget plan:

Monthly Income Received		
Date	Categories *(Source of funds)*	Amount

C – cash
D – debit
Chk – check
MO – money order

Categories	Amount Due	Amount Paid	Date	Form of Pmt. C/D/Chk/MO	Balance
TITHES /OFFERING					
MORTGAGE / RENT					
HOMEOWNERS INS.					
TAXES					
HOME MAINTENANCE					
GAS / ELECTRIC					
WATER					
GROCERIES					
TELEPHONE					
TRANSPORTATION					
AUTO INSURANCE					
GASOLINE					
LIFE INSURANCE					
HEALTH / DENTAL					
PRESCRIPTIONS					
CHILD / AFTER SCHOOL CARE					
EDUCATION EXP.					

Categories	Amount Due	Amount Paid	Date	Form of Pmt. C/D/Chk/MO	Balance
CABLE / INTERNET					
CLEANERS / LAUNDRY					
CLOTHING EXPENSE					
CREDIT CARD:					
CREDIT CARD:					
CREDIT CARD:					
MISC. EXPENSE:					
MISC. EXPENSE:					
MISC. EXPENSE:					
FAMILY HAIR CARE					
CELL PHONE:					
ENTERTAINMENT					
PUBLICATIONS / MAGAZINES					
SAVINGS / STOCK CONTRIBUTION					
TOTAL MONTHLY EXPENSES					

Record account reference and/or payment confirmation information and form of payment made:

Payment Categories	Account / Ref. / Confirmation #	Check #

Ending monthly balance: _____

DAILY EXPENDITURE: *WEEK 42 - 69*

Continue to maintain a daily expenditure log:

Example

Date	Categories	Amount Paid	+ / -	Form of Pmt. C/D/Chk/MO	Balance
7/18	Bowling	35.00	-	C	$10,350
	- Work Outing				10,315

Date	Categories	Amount Paid	+ / -	Form of Pmt. C/D/Chk/MO	Balance
		ENDING MONTHLY BALANCE			

C – cash   D – debit/credit   Chk – check   MO – money order

BUDGET: *MONTH 3 – WEEK 42 – 69*

Continue to follow the monthly budget plan:

Monthly Income Received		
Date	**Categories** *(Source of funds)*	**Amount**

C – cash
D – debit
Chk – check
MO – money order

Categories	Amount Due	Amount Paid	Date	Form of Pmt. C/D/Chk/MO	Balance
TITHES /OFFERING					
MORTGAGE / RENT					
HOMEOWNERS INS.					
TAXES					
HOME MAINTENANCE					
GAS / ELECTRIC					
WATER					
GROCERIES					
TELEPHONE					
TRANSPORTATION					
AUTO INSURANCE					
GASOLINE					
LIFE INSURANCE					
HEALTH / DENTAL					
PRESCRIPTIONS					
CHILD / AFTER SCHOOL CARE					
EDUCATION EXP.					

Categories	Amount Due	Amount Paid	Date	Form of Pmt. C/D/Chk/MO	Balance
CABLE / INTERNET					
CLEANERS / LAUNDRY					
CLOTHING EXPENSE					
CREDIT CARD:					
CREDIT CARD:					
CREDIT CARD:					
MISC. EXPENSE:					
MISC. EXPENSE:					
MISC. EXPENSE:					
FAMILY HAIR CARE					
CELL PHONE:					
ENTERTAINMENT					
PUBLICATIONS / MAGAZINES					
SAVINGS / STOCK CONTRIBUTION					
TOTAL MONTHLY EXPENSES					

Record account reference and/or payment confirmation information and form of payment made:

Payment Categories	Account / Ref. / Confirmation #	Check #

Ending monthly balance: _____

TIME MANAGEMENT

Mastering good time management skills will help you recognize where you waste time and allow you to find areas of your life where you don't spend enough time. The goal of the following time management techniques is to show you what you can do to change or successfully improve your time organization pattern.

#7

Maintain an attitude of self-assurance in knowing your life's purpose.

With good time management skills, you will be in control of your time, your life, of your stress and energy levels. You will make progress in most areas of daily life task. You will be able to maintain balance between your work, personal, and family life. You will have enough flexibility to respond to surprises or new opportunities.

All time management skills are learnable. More than likely you will see much improvement from simply becoming aware of the essence and causes of common personal time management problems. With the following time management techniques, you can see better which time management techniques are most relevant for your situation.

Just get started with them. Many of your problems will gradually disappear.

If you already know how you should be managing your time, but you still don't do it, don't give up. What you may be overlooking is the psychological side of your time management skills, psychological obstacles hidden behind your personality.

Depending on your personal situation, such obstacles may be the primary reason why you procrastinate, have difficulties saying no, delegating, or making time management decisions.

The psychological component of your time management skills can also be dealt with. The time management skills information on the following pages will point out relevant solution for most situations.

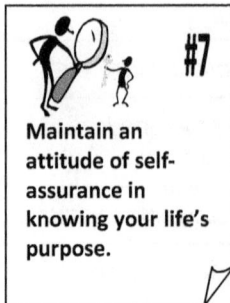

Getting past the psychological barrier

Have you ever tried to convince anyone to change their view of him- or herself? Was it easy? Everyone at one point or another often feels resistance to receiving outside opinions of our personality or habits. It is much easier to accept a change if we discover things for ourselves, if the opinion is our own.

Something similar happens with time spending habits. When you discover how you really spend your time, and do it yourself from your own time log, you will feel much more comfortable when changing your time management attitudes and habits.

Time tracking with a time log is much more than just a boring exercise in book keeping. If you approach it right, it will become a very effective time organization learning tool. A few minutes of writing and analyzing your time and activity logs will eliminate many hours of wasted time. Embrace the reality of your personal time.

Unless this has already happen to you before, your time log will more than likely surprise you. You will see how much time is wasted in many unexpected ways. Often it appears that the busier you believe you are the more time you will end up wasting.

Another important discovery is how much time things really take. One of the most common problems in personal time management is underestimating the time needed for each specific activity. First this is one of the reasons why planning and scheduling do not seem to work well for some people. If you always expect much more than you can fit in your time, than writing plans and to do lists will simply get you frustrated.

Be realistic, visualize your time and you will feel much more in control. In fact, you will begin to find that you will move much faster and actually have less stress.

Preparing and writing your time log.

You don't need to keep a time log permanently. It is sufficient to create documentation, and then learn to establish a mental habit. A great time management tool is "The Visionary Journal", which has a section specifically for time management, it can be ordered at: www.appleseedpd.com/Publications.html.

When you create a time log, make sure you don't miss even the smallest activity. Most times you can easily overlook little time wasters, which can actually cause you to create delays in other areas. In order to begin learning how to identify and eliminate time waster take time to write out a tracking record. This process can easily be done by taking a sheet of paper and dividing it into the following columns:

• Date
• Activities (People associated w/activity)
• Time Allotted
• Priority Level

Document activities you would normally perform daily. Update your time log each time you switch to a new activity or at some short time intervals, like 10-20 minutes.
Add entries to your "Time Allotted" and "Activities" column, and be sure to note priority level, and where relevant, make short notes on what people you spend time with too.

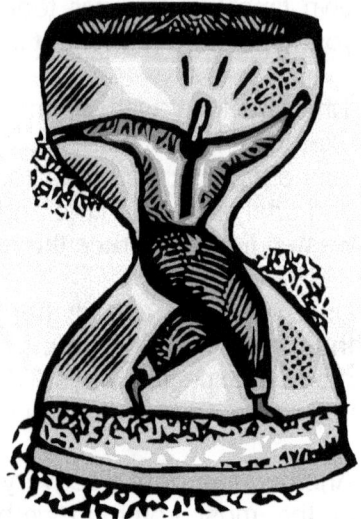

Over the next couple of weeks get in a habit of creating a priority list for tasks you need to accomplish throughout your day and week. Use the following activity time table as a guideline to follow for future task management and assessment of daily priorities.

- - -

TIME MANAGEMENT ACTIVITY LOG: DAY 14 - 69

Date	Activity	Time Allotted	Priority Level 1 2 3 4

SOCIAL INTERACTION / HEALTHY RELATIONSHIPS

Study after study has proven that spending time with family and friends, and establishing healthy relationships is essential and viable to attaining better health an overall quality of life.

Mastering Leverage
Healthy social interaction and relationship steam from developmental roots. Depending upon environmental exposure to social interaction in earlier years would determine how an individual develop an ability to interact socially with others as an adult. Naturally, we cannot choose the family we are birthed into. Understood, based on environmental dynamics would then nine times out of ten shape our social perspective. Based on the make-up of the family origin will help create the psychological behavioral patterns of how both men and women will relate to one another and learn a communication structure.

Dependent upon those factors would then innately determine one's ability to master a skill called leverage. Learning how to create social leverage is a skill that simply allows an individual to take on the responsibility of getting something done. Relative to one's belief that whatever situation requires a decision to be made, they have the knowledge and leadership mindset to navigate the outcome. This position however, should also be coupled with balance. If the skill of leverage is mastered it will be an asset in both personal and business relationships established.

What would necessitate the need for leverage in relationship exactly? If an individual takes on the methodology of mastering leverage they will also learn how to agree with a situation, even when they disagree. This dual role is called compromise. Compromise and balance are key components to establishing healthy relationships. How can two walk together, except they agree? Men and women have areas of necessary development when it comes to the social knack of taking into account that question. Although the answer is simple, being confident and strongly understanding what your level of compromise may be integrating leverage to find a balanced middle ground will successfully determine the final result.

Recognizing Healthy and Unhealthy Relationships
The complex nature of social situations makes it difficult for one to isolate their self from social interaction and establishment of

relationship. However, settling for just a desire to incorporate any type of companionship is not wise, and can invite unhealthy relationships.

It is important to be wise when establishing friendships, and/or relationships, don't be hasty and understand the purpose. Using good judgment when creating the friendship can alleviate unhealthy entanglement with a "fool" so-to-speak.

Unhealthy relationships can be considered toxic in nature. When something is termed toxic it can be poisonous or even deadly. A toxic relationship can be harmful to the overall well being of an individual. Ultimately, establishing unhealthy relationships or entertaining unnecessary social interactions can cause contamination to once purposeful good habits. Concluding, how can an individual judge a healthy relationship versus an unhealthy relationship? Clearly, using wisdom and god-given discernment at the onset or even while in the relationship and identifying the motive.

The Dynamics of Men & Women Working Together

On several occasions it has been heard by millions from pulpits and public platforms the importance of learning how to agree even when you do not agree. It is an interesting concept to use, but it will take patience and understanding in order to handle such a notable suggestion. I recall a nice eloquently spoken story given by a Pastor pertaining to the complexity of a relationship between a husband and wife. After analyzing the story, I was easily able to incorporate it into day-to-day intertwining with even social networking experiences between opposite sexes.

The Story

A couple walked into a Pastor's office to discuss difficulty they were undergoing in their marriage. Upon the entry of their meeting with the Pastor, he cleverly placed toys on his desk as the couple proceeded to sit down. He placed a doll and a small tea set on the side of his desk where the wife sat, and a Tonka Truck and G.I. Joe men on the side of the desk where the husband sat.

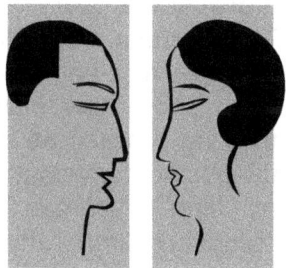

The wife began to go into relaying her side of the story, and as she began to talk, unbeknownst she simultaneously picked-up the doll that was on the desk. She began stating how her husband does not spend much time talking or communicating with her. "He is either working or sleeping, and it has become an absolute annoyance in my life" the wife said.

The husband started shaking his head and saying, "I can't believe how she is complaining about I don't talk to her. I mean, I go to work, I pay the bills, I take care of her needs, and all I expect of her is to take care of the children and allow me to have time to myself when I want to watch a football game. I have never asked her to work, I don't even ask her to cook if she doesn't feel like it, and I pay a housekeeper once a month if she tells me too. So, honestly, I don't know what her grip is all about!"

The Pastor smiled and began to ask the question: "Wife, when you were a child, just as you are holding the doll in your hand right now, did you also like to play with dolls and tea sets when you were a little girl?" The wife responded: "Yes, of course, and I loved having my tea parties, but what does that have to do with me being a woman and a wife to him now?"

The Pastor then grinned again, and proceeded to ask the husband: "Did you notice the Tonka truck and G.I. Joe men?" The husband sighed and said: "Yeah Pastor." The Pastor then went on to ask the question: "When you played with your G-I-Joe men, and I am sure you also had cars and trucks to play with to, did you make noise like you were raving-up the engines on your trucks and cars then clashing the G.I. Joe men back and forth like they were going to battle?" The husband then said: "Of course, don't all little kids (boys) go through that phase at one-point or another in their young childhood?"

Moral of the Story
The Pastor's response was quite simple, he gave a word of advice: "Compromise and balance… the whole purpose of the illustrated toys is to show how instinctively a man and woman starts out their thinking process as a child. By nature a woman will enjoy graceful things and conversation, which is all a part of her emotional make-up by birth. Whereas, a man may generally outwit his way of communicating, through action, an expression of indirect communication, this in actuality is all part of a man's natural structure and demeanor."

The simple truth is learning how to establish an understanding and medium between the two individuals. Even though the wife desires to be talked to, the husband's way of talking is taking care of what he believes her needs are so that he won't necessarily have to hear any complaints. However, establishing a mutual understanding of both forms of communication is a desire that both individuals should have, in order to create balance and resolution.

Point Taken
Even though women by nature can be considered emotional creatures, it is important not to be emotionally messy. Getting a handle or taking control over your ability to become confident in any situation is essential, when intertwining with a spouse or people in general. Women should have the ability to command a presence, which is simply establishing a confident self-assurance of who you know you are as a human being! Once a certain level of confidence is obtained, balancing leverage in communication will become easy.

From birth men are raised to be a dominate force, taking on a mindset of having a sense of control. However, the significant factor in this truth is having the ability to maintain balance and control at the same time. Men naturally do not like to be pushed or backed into an imbalanced state; rather they desire to go head-on with whatever situation comes their way. They have the mindset that "I can handle it– let me!"

If in fact men lived on an island that mindset may actually work, but in the case of mastering leverage in social business or personal relationships, men will need to become skilled in the rules of the game. A more balanced equation would cause a man to recognize that the sole objective in playing the life balancing game is simply leveraging the playing field an incorporating a (1+1=2) or (2 is > than 1) team-player instinct. Men can always believe they are a leader, even if they need to make a decision to compromise being in the order of second position.

Leveraging Key Principle:		
Cooperation	Give	
Negotiation	**+** Take	**=** *A Well Balanced Compromise*

On the following pages write out plans of action as to how you believe you can improve your decision making process as it relates to acknowledging the difference between healthy and unhealthy relationships. Also determine how you can create leverage in social networking interactions and time you set aside to spend with family and friends.

Developing Social Networking / Relationship Goals
DAY 14 - 69

Develop goals you desire to use as a guideline to create leverage and balance in social, family, friends and personal relationships:

Goal #	Action Plan
1	
2	
3	
4	
5	
6	

Over the next couple of weeks establish a checks and balancing list that will depict a comparison between unhealthy and healthy relationships you are involved in. Describe how the relationship was formulated and why it may be considered an asset or may turn out to be an unfruitful liability in your life.

Relationship: Healthy vs. Unhealthy	Asset	Liability	Why?

Recognizing Healthy vs. Unhealthy Relationships (conti.)

Relationship: Healthy vs. Unhealthy	Asset	Liability	Why?

Create an 8-week or weekly event calendar that would detail: outings, vacation, dinner with family and friends, and social networking events.

DATE / TIME:	EVENT:
DETAILS:	

DATE / TIME:	EVENT:
DETAILS:	

Document details pertaining to outings, vacation, dinner with family and friends, and social networking events.

DATE / TIME:	EVENT:
DETAILS:	

DATE / TIME:	EVENT:
DETAILS:	

DATE / TIME:	EVENT:
DETAILS:	

DATE / TIME:	EVENT:
DETAILS:	

DATE / TIME:	EVENT:
DETAILS:	

DATE / TIME:	EVENT:
DETAILS:	

Personal goal planning is extremely important when also handling your personal time management. Your life is a sequence of big and small choices and decisions, once you decide what you want it is those choices that you ultimately really must take control over and manage. It is important to pursue learning how to work from your goals, instead of simply just setting them. You must be courageous enough to go directly to a goal you have created in your mind, and work your way back mentally to the conceptual core and starting point.

Personal goal planning is the wisdom that comes out of a lot of practical experience and psychological research to help you direct your conscious and subconscious decisions towards success, building up your motivation to achieve your ambitious life goals. Goal setting is a course of action you can take to demonstrate written plans of decisions you will make. Time and time again it has been said that people who set goals are more successful than people who don't.

You can establish a good goal setting system by using principles defined in our "DREAM" goal planning guidelines:

- Declaration
- Realistic
- Eclectic
- Attainable
- Measureable

If you neglect establishing wise realistic goals, the odds that your goals will be achieved will become less probable. Why?

The key force that either drives you towards your goals or holds you back is your unconscious mindset. We have discovered that our "DREAM" goal planning strategies are necessary for maintaining focus in your subconscious mind. To accept your goals and allow them to start budding, without strategic planning, you will find that you will become easily distracted and most times stay in the comfort zone of your present conditions and maintain old habits.

Once you declare a goal, make sure it is realistic. Then be eclectic in your thinking, meaning be sure not to confine your goal planning to one point of view. Learn to manifest brilliance in your thinking patterns, (be éclat). From the very beginning when declaring your goals, speak out that it is attainable. Lastly, use wisdom when creating a method of measurability, to ensure your continuous focus towards achieving the goal.

Declaration

When you declare goals you can clearly see a direction you want to follow, and you have certain standards that you intend to pursue in order to achieve your goals. In making decisions to declare your goals, it is important that you actually write them first, which is crucial in all goal planning.

The more precise your goal is, the more realistic your success will be, and the shorter the path you need to take will become. When you visualize, speak out and write down goals your unconscious thinking will be outweighed by possible procrastinating distractions that may arise.

Realistic

A realistic goal is a practical pathway to follow that will lead to optimum achievement. Recognized logical premise will be established along the way. This does not mean that the lower you aim the more likely you will be in reaching success. It is well known that goals that work best can be hard work and will have some challenging times. Many times we chose ambitious goals, but they should still be realistic, then you will be more motivated to stay on track. Research critical elements of goals you desire in order to maximize your success in obtaining them.

Eclectic

Brainstorming is a bold effort to take on when you set out to pursue goals. When you choose to create possible options for reaching your goals, you take limits off of the possibility if one route does not completely go as planned, you have a plan B you will follow. Being eclectic in your thinking will allow you to be better prepared when 'oops' occurs or you run into a dead end. A good goal planner will strategically know how to make a quick turn in another direction before completely reaching a 'halting stop' in their well thought-out plans of action.

Attainable

A goal can be attainable when you have clear reasons why you want to reach that goal. This is one more place where it is important that the goal is realistic. Prepare specific reasons and expected outcomes in writing. Visualization of attaining desired goals is key to keeping you motivated to achieving them. Every time you get stuck and don't feel motivated enough, read over your original declaration and walk out your end results in your mind. This is a very powerful practical technique of how to get through difficult moments and not quit.

Measurability Timetable

For a goal to be capable of being measured, you need a way to strategize your progress and follow a plan that will estimate when you will achieve your goal. Documenting progress is very important for you to stay motivated and enjoy going through the process of reaching the goal.

When you make wise realistic goals it is important to set a specific timeline. This is also very important for your unconscious thinking. Time is the price you pay for the attainable goal you desire to achieve. Setting the deadline will protect you from paying a higher price than the goal is worth. This is also your protection from procrastination and perfectionism.

- - -

Over the next couple of weeks write out a declaration of goals you desire to achieve. Use measuring guidelines in order to strategize how you will reach the goals you set-out to reach. Make sure your goals are realistic, so that you can maintain a level of motivation. Once you meet each measuring level you will feel as though your goals are worthwhile in continuing to reach them until you achieve them. Create a manageable timetable in order to make sure you are performing daily tasks towards your goals.

- - -

Briefly create some projected goals below: *Day 14 - 69*

3-Month Projection Goals

Month	Desired Goal

Month	Desired Goal

Month	Desired Goal

8-Week Projected Goals

Week 1	Weekly Goal

Week 2	Weekly Goal

Week 3	Weekly Goal

Week 4	Weekly Goal

Week 5	Weekly Goal

Week 6	Weekly Goal

Week 7	Weekly Goal

Week 8	Weekly Goal

"You must train yourself to see your end from the beginning, decide on the course of direction you will take, then "Go For The Goal!"

#8

Prepare a realistic navigation process and you will avoid many obstacles along the way.

Over the last couple of weeks, you should have experienced improvement in your decision-making process, through learning how to create balance in six-core life areas. Use the next seven days to take time to review and summarize steps you took to organize and establish a daily systematic method. Focus on how you can continue to implement techniques you acquired as you strive towards completion of your 90-day "Life Reboot."

DELETE

Make the determination that you will obtain the results,
you have always desired by completely relinquishing all
the hindrances you once had just days ago . . .

Day: 78 ~ 82

DELETE

Delete means to remove or make something disappear.
- **Erase:** *to remove or destroy completely*
- **Edit, expunge**: *cut or eliminate*

Now that you have identified places of complacency in your life, and have learned how to make alterations in your decision-making process. The next step is being bold enough to create a check off list that will guide you towards moving past areas of your life that you once allowed to be limitations or obstacles.

A difficult place to be in at times is a 'comfort zone'. Why? Simple, these places in our lives have the undeniable ability to cause contentment. Of course, one could say, what is wrong with being happy or satisfied where you are? The answer: "There is absolutely no harm in being satisfied where you are, however, if you have allowed limitations to dictate your ability to move forward, or continuously have growth in your life, then, being satisfied is not acceptable." If you are living, you should also pursue to maintain a consistent desire to keep growing as well.

Growth is the process of expanding or developing. A life well lived will show a pattern of budding in whatever point of life you are in. Once an individual has mastered the ability to command a certain direction in life they desire to take, there is absolutely little room for complacency to take place. Certain people in your life may be a root cause for placing you in a mindset of content. A job that offers no room for growth, a lack of time management or establishing realistic goals may also be the cause of unproductive growth evolving in your life.

Grasping hold of the tools you have discovered through organizing and re-evaluating what is at the core of how you make decisions pertaining to your daily living is intricately important. In order to successfully understand how to uproot old or unfruitful seeds that you once planted, get serious about the process of elimination. When you make up your mind that every day of your life will end with daily expectations being met with no regrets, then choosing to delete all hindrances and barriers in your pathway is a decision you must make.

Having a new mindset to completely tear down any tangible obstacle that posse opposition in your path is a bold stand to take on. However, when you have concluded that you are tired of being "stuck" in unproductive places in your life, it is well worth the effort to take on a 'no tolerant attitude', that will ultimately push you into a position, that will re-route you in a better direction.

TIME TO DELETE

Acknowledge all the hindering areas in your life you are ready to literally delete, in order to experience total transformation and abundant living.

What areas in your life are you now able to completely move pass?

_____

_____

_____

_____

_____

What areas of your life do you know may take a little time to dissolve, but will in the near future?

_____

_____

_____

_____

_____

What areas of your life do you know will be more productive after you move beyond the hindrances once created?

_____

_____

_____

_____

_____

#9

Be motivated, encouraged and determined to excel beyond your greatest expectations.

Now that your action plans are written, you can move to the most important part, the analysis. Looking over your life wheel, daily journals, financial management, time and goal planning logs, and how you establish healthy relationships, what have you learned about your decision making process?

Analyze the percentage of time you spent in each of the different core areas of your life. Depending on how you divided your time between spiritual growth, handling finances, establishing relationships, spending time with family, goal planning, and overall fitness, answer the following questions:

- What percentage of your activities was most unproductive?

- What percentages of your activities are urgent?

- What core area have you spent the most of your time?

- What percentages of your activities usually went as planned?

- What are main interruptions and/or distractions?

- What are the activities you will cut back on?

- What activities will you delegate or simplify?

- What steps can you establish to hold yourself accountable?

BREAKING BAD HABITS

When we invent reasons why we feel as though we're unable to move past certain situations, life patterns or circumstances, we build barriers that will eventually block opportunities. Taking control over our thoughts and deciding how we can alter our decisions will determine our ability to break through the strongholds we actually create in our life. The following are examples of real life scenarios or rather excuses that people make for allowing core areas of their life to become "stuck".

Examples:
- I don't set aside a specific time to pray in the mornings, so I just pray when I can. However I know that if I do pray I would more times than not get better results in whatever situation I am faced with.
- I over spend when I go to the market, because I usually don't have discipline myself to write out a list before going shopping.
- I do wish I could establish healthy relationships, but because I don't want to be alone, I just settle for whoever comes my way.
- I do desire to use my time more wisely, but I don't establish priorities because my life is too busy right now!
- I do have a hobby that I could actually turn into a business, but I haven't taken time to research how to strategically put together a business plan.
- I seem to always look forward to starting a new diet when Monday comes, but by the end of the day, I tend to fall off, and say I will start over next week, because I don't prepare meals beforehand.
- The process to my financial freedom is complicated so I have not taken the time to create a budget just yet.

Take time to put your faith into action and document bad habits that must be broken and completely deleted from your life.

CORE AREA	HABITS THAT WILL BE BROKEN
Fitness/Health	I don't like to exercise.

CORE AREA	HABITS THAT WILL BE BROKEN

Review areas that you have pin-pointed as bad habits. Then determine how you can re-focus and progress towards steps to help you re-evaluate your decision making process.

RE-FOCUS: DAY 79

#10
When you have done your very best, stretch to do even better.

"But let him ask in faith, nothing wavering. For he that wavereth is like a wave of the sea driven with the wind and tossed… A double minded man is unstable in all his ways." – James 1:6;8

Faith is building blocks that every individual must have in order to continuously grow. It is a belief system that every human being should use as inner trust in something that may or may not have any logical proof. Faith is imperative to ignite before making any decisions, mainly because if you don't have faith in what you believe, and stand on the decisions you make, you will waver on decisions at one point you felt confident about.

Effectively exercising your faith (your foundational building blocks) will help you build certainty to break-through any "stuck" areas in your life or decision-making process. Therefore as you reviewed hindering bad habits you have chosen to completely delete / dismiss in your life, by faith choose to not be double minded and pick them back up again.

Building on principles of faith, and implementing sound judgment to determine desired outcomes is what will allow you to maintain balance in decisions you choose. When you make decisions, you choose to accept whatever the ending result may be. Based on the premise that you were able to centralize on areas that had gotten out of control, and you have desired to make necessary alterations to determine priorities, you have now ultimately place yourself in a much better position to make decisions with no regrets.

Following is an example of a decision-making tree, essentially it is a diagram that represents, in an organized way, the decisions and the main external or other events that introduce uncertainty, as well as possible results of all possible decisions and events. The diagram is a schematic example that illustrates how a decision making process can unfold.

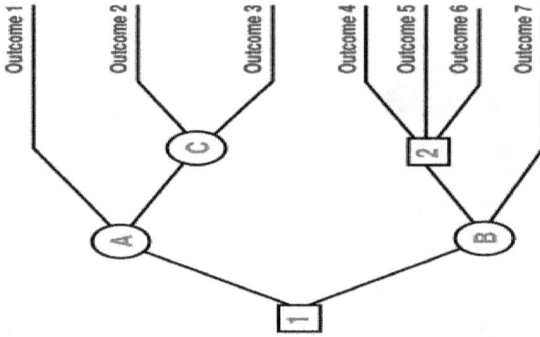

☐ - Decisions   ◯ - Uncertain Decisions

Squares represent decisions you can make. The lines that branch out of each square represent all the available possible results/outcomes that can be selected at the decision analysis point.

Circles show various circumstances that have uncertain outcomes (For example, some types of events that may affect you on a given path). The lines that branch out of each circle indicate possible outcomes of the uncertain decisions.

Create a decision tree that represents a decision you are currently faced with, and then use as many probabilities as you like to show how you rate your decision, for example: if you have eight possible outcomes rate each uncertain decision in the order of greatest to least: ("80% - favorable" or "0.8–not sure"). Put number values in squares, and letter values in circles.

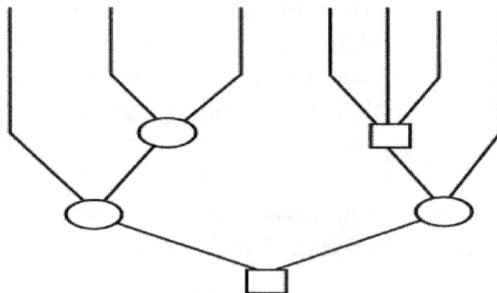

Each path that can be followed along the decision tree from left to right, will led to a specific result. You need to describe those end results in terms of your main decisive factor for judging the results of your decisions. Ideally, you will assign each end result a quantitative measure of the overall total benefit you will receive from that outcome.

Now you have a complete decision making tree with specific numbers for both the probabilities of the uncertain events and the benefit measures (desirability) of each end result. At this stage the tree can give you more specific recommendation on what would be your best choices.

In particular, for each choice that you control (at the decision points shown by squares), you can calculate the overall desirability of that choice. Just sum the benefit measures of all the end outcomes that can be traced back to that choice (via one path or another), weighted by the probabilities of the corresponding paths. This will show you the preferred choice (the one with the highest overall desirability).

If you have more than one decision point, you need to do an accurate calculation for the decisions that are at the latest stages first. Identify the choice that gives the highest overall desirability and leave only that branch (removing the decision point). Do the same with the remaining squares, working your way to the left (to the first decision point in the sequence).

In an effort to create a process of elimination, you can use this tool as a guide or mapping process for other decisions you need to basically weigh out. However, remember the most important key to the overall process is first lining up your faith through prayer, believing that whatever the end result, it will be the ideal choice.

– – –

RE-EVALUATE: DAY 80 – 81

Focusing on a "Decision Making Process" allows someone the ability to know how to consistently make decisions while maintaining balance in their core values and beliefs. When a door of opportunity confronts you, don't be afraid to open it, believe that the sky is the limit. Walk in prudence and by faith, believing you are more equipped to implementing balance in making decisions.

Re-evaluate how wise you have become with mastering your decision-making process, through using the final evaluation tool. Rate your response from 1 being uncertain, to 5 being absolutely certain.

Statement	1	2	3	4	5
1 When I make a decision, I determine or evaluate the risk that may go along with it.	○	○	○	○	○
2 Usually, after I make a decision, I am okay and feel strong about my choice.	○	○	○	○	○
3 I do try to analyze most situations, before even beginning a decision-making process.	○	○	○	○	○
4 When I come up with a solution to a problem, I mostly rely on my own judgment.	○	○	○	○	○

5	My decisions are usually based on faith and logical inner instinct about the problem or situation at hand.	○	○	○	○	○
6	Consequences derived from my decisions made, I am usually fine with, but sometimes regretful.	○	○	○	○	○
7	I have the ability to make sound decisions, and tend to assure myself through the process of making it.	○	○	○	○	○
8	When I look to others to give me assistance with making a decision, I often find that things can get a little complicated.	○	○	○	○	○
9	When I am in doubt about a decision I need to make, I will re-evaluate possible outcomes.	○	○	○	○	○
10	Making a decision can sometimes take time for me, because I will analyze what tools are best to use.	○	○	○	○	○
11	I do consider at times alternative solutions to decisions I need to make, plan A and plan B.	○	○	○	○	○
12	I determine how I will implement my decision, before I share my thoughts with anyone.	○	○	○	○	○
13	In a group decision-making process, when I am the team leader I tend to consider other ideas, but most times successfully get team to buy into my idea as a collaborative effort.	○	○	○	○	○
14	I use rational judgment about my audience before I share my decision with others.	○	○	○	○	○
15	Rarely, I find it hard to discuss a decision I have made when I know it may impact another person harshly.	○	○	○	○	○
16	I will stand firm and make a decision that I will not allow others to talk me out of.	○	○	○	○	○

17	I determine factors that are a priority in my decision-making process, and then use my determination of priorities to evaluate outcomes.	⌀	⌀	⌀	⌀	⌀
18	When I want others to buy into my decisions, I will emphatically insist that I have made a wise choice.	⌀	⌀	⌀	⌀	⌀
		Total =				

Score Interpretation

Score	Comment
18-42	Regardless of what you are making a decision on, you are not goal-oriented enough, and you rely too much on chance, instinct or timing to make reliable decisions. Start to improve your decision-making skills by focusing more on establishing goals that will lead to sound decisions, rather than on simply the decision itself. Review the "alteration" portion of the book, to establish a more solid process, so you will learn to face any decision with confidence.
43-66	Your decision-making process is average. You have a good understanding of core elements, but now you need to improve your process and be more proactive. Concentrate on finding lots of options and discovering as many risks and consequences as you can. The better your analysis, the better your decision will be in the long term. Focus specifically on the areas where you are not as strong in, and develop a system that will work for you across a wide variety of situations: Financial, Spiritual, Goal-Planning, Time Management, Physical, and Social Networking.
67-90	You have an excellent approach to decision-making! You know how to set up the process and generate lots of potential solutions. From there, you analyze the options carefully, and you make the best decisions possible based on what you know. As you gain more and more experience, use that information to evaluate your decisions, and continue to build on your decision-making success. Think about the areas where you lost points, and decide how you can include those areas in your process.

RE-DESIGN: DAY 82

As you answered the questions, did you see some commonality in the way you have chosen to make decisions in the past? The quiz was based on six essential steps in the decision-making process:

#12 Train your ear to hear, eyes to see, and mind to contain fruitful life accomplishments.

1. Establishing a optimistic decision-making environment.
2. Generating possible resolutions.
3. Evaluating options.
4. Deciding.
5. Checking the decision.
6. Communicating and implementing.

If you master these six basic elements and improve the way you structure them, this will help you to continually develop a better overall decision-making system. Let's look at the six elements individually.

Establishing a Positive Decision-Making Environment
If you've ever been in a situation where you were looked to determine a outcome, then you've experienced what the decision-making environment can be when established. It is important to be clear on the bases of your objectives on issues you are expected to make a decision on. This includes agreeing on a plan that would cause you to move your well thought decision forward. You may have an opportunity to operate this tool when dealing with friends, family, co-workers, in social interactions, or even deciding to completely dismiss unproductive situations.

Generating Possible Resolutions
Another important part of a good decision process is learning to count up the cost as to how the decisions you make will impact other areas of your life. If you simply accept the first solution you come up with, then you may overlook a possible better option. Having the ability to execute due diligence and look at various perspectives to your choice will allow you to make a wise decision.

Evaluating Options

The stage of exploring alternatives is often the most time-consuming part of the decision-making process. This stage sometimes takes so long that a decision is never made! To make this step efficient, be clear about the factors you want to include in your analysis. There are three key factors to consider:

1. **Risk** – Most decisions involve some risk. However, as we discussed in Altering (Goal Planning) portion of this book you learned how to uncover and override possible risks and/or distractions in order to make the best choice possible.

2. **Results** – You can't project the implications of a decision with 100% accuracy. But you can use faith, be prayerful, careful and organized in the way you approach and evaluate possible results.

3. **Attainability** – Is the choice realistic and implementable? This factor is often ignored. You usually have to consider certain constraints when making a decision. As part of this evaluation stage, ensure that the alternative you've selected is significantly better than the other options, but will be attainable. Ultimately you will need to decide on a checks and balance of what you will control, can alter or completely determine deletion through a process of elimination.

Deciding

Making a decision in itself can be exciting and stressful. To help you deal with these emotions as objectively as possible, use a structured approach to the decision making process. This means taking a look at what's most important in the decision you need to make. Take the time to think ahead and determine exactly what will make the decision "right." This will significantly improve your decision accuracy.

Checking the Decision

Remember that whatever you have determined is at your core when balancing decisions, some things about a decision are not purposed. You should pray about the decision, have faith and conclude that it makes sense on a perceptive and natural level as well. Once you are certain and confident as to how you handle making decisions, it will be imperative to check alternatives you chose for validity and "delete" options that simply do not "make sense."

If a decision is a significant one, it is also worth assessment to make sure that by faith your assumptions are clear, and that the well-thought structure you use to make decisions is wise.

Communicating and Implementing

The last stage in the decision-making process involves communicating your choice and preparing to implement it. You can try to implement your decision-making process on others by demanding their acceptance. Or you can gain others acceptance by incorporating good communication skills through your mastery of social leverage, as you learned in your prior reading within the "Altering" phase of "Making The Decision".

Establish a plan for implementing your decisions utilizing exemplified social interaction practices. Be assertive yet wise when handing over your well thought through decisions on matters to others. Also, be bold enough to choose to discard decisions that do not line up accurately with what is right.

Key Points

Decision-making is a skill – and skills can usually be improved. As you have gained knowledge through reading "Making the Decision" – to Reboot Your Life", you now have experience in a clear pattern of how to make wiser decisions. As you become more familiar with applying the tools and structures needed for effective decision-making, you'll improve your confidence.

You can extend your decision making options by pursuing to obtain an accountability partner. You may also decide to subscribe to Appleseed Accountability Partner News, where you can request to receive information on certain subject matters that will help you to continue to stay on track for maintaining goals: http://www.appleseedpd.com/
Accountability-Partner-News.html.

Take the opportunity to think about how you have improved your decision-making process and steps you have learned to take your skills to the next level. Ultimately, through improving your decision-making skills you are recharged, refocused and ready to create a deletion check off list.

-   -   -

DELETE: CHECK OFF LIST

Besides determining bad habits you need to break, the check off list you will create below should further depict all other areas of your life you have chosen to completely detach, discard, uproot and simply dismiss from being a part of your future . . .

First, determine why you have made this choice; second be clear about the necessity to move forward from this point. Lastly, be bold, precise, transparent and adamant about making this decision, without wavering.

You may need to choose to detach yourself from people that you have allowed to be distractions. Certain influential people may be friends, colleagues, associates or even someone you have considered significant. You must be honest enough with yourself to know that not everyone you choose to surround yourself with is purposed to play an intricate role in your life.

Discard or rid clutter in your home or things that simply do not operate productively any more. Choose to uproot tendencies that have triggered down-spiraling lingering attachments as well. Every stronghold that stands in your path of moving forward is a burden you do not have to entertain. You can make a decision to completely delete any limitation that posse opposition. Finally, fearlessly dismiss any and all thoughts of defeat in every area of your life. When this task is complete you will be prepared and ready to reboot your future.

Let's begin the deletion process!

Check-off List		
√	Area Of Deletion	Details

Check-off List (continued)		
√	Area Of Deletion	Details

You have wisely and boldly accomplished a courageous task in completely dismissing and choosing to live a more abundant life by laying aside every weight of hindrance. Now, consider lying down to "Sleep" ask yourself two questions: "Can I go to bed tonight with a clear heart and mind (conscious) and live with the decisions I have made with no regrets?" Also, "can I be assured that areas of my life I have chosen to delete and move pass pertaining to both personal stagnation or involving others is absolutely the best decision I have ever made?" If you have confidently answered both questions with an absolute "yes", then you are ready to begin re-booting your life.

REBOOT

. . .

Day: 83 ~ 90

REBOOT

The commitment you initiated 82 days ago to create change in your life was worth every dedicated day you implemented new ways to handle daily life decisions. Today, you're no longer attempting to figure out how to connect the dots or redirect your path, you made it! You have learned successful keys to establishing a life of balance. You chose to reboot your life and now you have literally re-loaded a new way of operating a previously failed system or systematic way of doing something. You made the decision to begin a new process, and you now have the power and opportunity to move forward with momentum.

The second and final step once you press the reboot button is to use the principles learned and apply it to the rest of your everyday life. Depending upon how well you stuck to daily plans of action through the last 82-days will determine how you can best apply or show acknowledgement that you have obtained answers to a better way of living. You should be able to walk in confidence as well as feel empowered and encouraged to exercise your new success to the fullest. Think about how you can now plant seeds in the lives of others by sharing this new found knowledge of successful living.

Your successful tools of knowledge obtained can efficiently be shared with others by creating a synopsis of steps you have learned. Within the next couple of pages document new revised blueprints of your daily tasks. Decisions you have mastered on how to skillfully navigate through daily tasks will be similar to designing a treasure map of how you ultimately reached your goal.

TREASURE MAP BLUEPRINTS: DAY 83 - 89

Re-Boot Your New Life Blueprints!

Now that you are starting a new journey; each day will be lived in abundance. Over the next 7 days, using the six-core areas of life techniques you have mastered, follow the steps of the **7-day** guidelines to create a tryout of what your New Life Blueprints will entail.

Day 1: Before executing any plans in your day, every morning you should have an established set time for prayer, reflect and journal your thoughts.

Day 2: Write a vision and mission statement for your life and family. .

Day 3: Maintain your consistent fitness and dietary goals daily . . .

Day 4: Establish checks & balance system to manage your daily task.

Day 5: Document a healthy forecast of financial expectations you will achieve daily.

Day 6: Arrange to set aside time you expect to vacation, have dinner with family, friends, and attend social outings. You should make time also for social networking events you plan to attend.

Day 7: Create an actual map and blueprints of what your successful life will look like within the next 3 – 5 years, document desired goals and aspirations.

Do not accept procrastination any more to become center stage of any event you set-out to accomplish. Take the tools you have learned and use them as your guide to abundant living. Continue to listen to your wise and bold mental decision making processor for instructions and keep moving forward. . . Your vision and resourcefulness is going to be your greatest life asset.

Day 1 – "Life Reboot" Blueprints (Day 83)

Date: _____

Day: _____

Before executing any plans in your day, set
aside time to pray, reflect and journal your thoughts.

_____
_____
_____
_____
_____
_____
_____
_____
_____
_____
_____
_____
_____
_____
_____
_____
_____
_____
_____
_____

Day 2 – "Life Reboot" Blueprints (Day 84)

Date: _____

Day: _____

Write and review your vision and mission statement
for your life and family, daily . . . *(post it in an area where it will always
stay as a focused vision to obtain and mission to live by.)*

_____

_____

_____

_____

_____

_____

_____

_____

_____

_____

_____

_____

_____

_____

_____

_____

_____

_____

_____

_____

Day 3 – "Life Reboot" Blueprints (Day 85)

Date: _____

Day: _____

Maintain a healthy lifestyle: document your daily fitness and dietary goals. Journal any thoughts you have pertaining to your fitness expectations.

_____

_____

_____

_____

_____

_____

_____

_____

Create a tracking log of your daily food menu and measurements. Your log should show a healthy eating pattern and fitness assessments.

Breakfast	
Lunch	
Dinner	
Exercise	Allotted Time: ____ Weight: ____
Measurements	Arms: Legs: Waist: Hips:

Day 4 – "Life Reboot" Blueprints (Day 86)

Date: _____

Day: _____

Be assertive and proactive: create a daily checks and balance system to manage your time.

✓	Activity	Time Allotted	Priority Level 1 2 3 4

Day 5 – "Life Reboot" Blueprints (Day 87)

Date: _____

Day: _____

Write out your daily financial forecast and expectations for the day.

Document current income balance below:

Income Received			
Date	Categories *(Source of funds)*	Amount	

Document all of your expenditures for the day. . .

Date	Categories	Amount Paid	+ / -	Form of Pmt. C/D/Chk/MO	Balance

Day 6 ~ "Life Reboot" Blueprints (Day 88)

Date: _____

Day: _____

Document special activities you will plan or will participate in with family and friends this week.

_____

_____

_____

DATE / TIME:	EVENT:
DETAILS:	

DATE / TIME:	EVENT:
DETAILS:	

Journal information pertaining to social events you plan to attend.
(Be sure to use the leveraging techniques you learned)

_____

_____

_____

_____

DATE / TIME:	EVENT:
DETAILS:	

Day 7 – "Life Reboot" Blueprints (Day 89)

Date: _____

Day: _____

TOTAL REBOOT: TRANSFORMATION

Based on the following six core areas on the life wheel using a scale from 1–10, where 1=unhappy and 10=completely satisfied, **how would you rate the balance in your life now?**

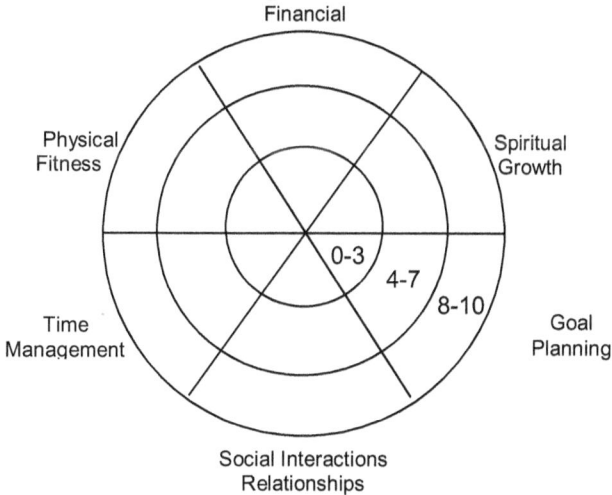

Financial

Physical Fitness

Spiritual Growth

0-3
4-7
8-10

Time Management

Goal Planning

Social Interactions Relationships

Your life wheel should be balanced or contain less areas of imbalance.

Using the DREAM goal planning guidelines you learned about in the previous "Altering" phase, allowed you to document anticipated goals and life pursuits you expect to accomplish within the next 3 -5 years.

You can accomplish this task by simply using a notebook, poster board or "The Visionary Goal Planner" that you can purchase from Appleseed Professional Development website: appleseedpd.com/Publications.html. This task will allow you to create a well thought out mapping process. Include the decisions you have so far already made that will point you in a clear direction of reaching your ultimate desired destiny.

VISUALIZATION & DECLARATION

Write out a brief vivid visual declaration of where you see yourself in the next 3-years.

_____
_____
_____
_____
_____
_____
_____
_____
_____
_____
_____
_____
_____
_____
_____
_____
_____
_____

Sign your name: Date: _____

Next, write out a brief declaration statement of a short-term goal you expect to accomplish within the next year.

DECLARATION STATEMENT

On this _____ day in the month of _____ in the year of: _____
I desire: _____
_____
_____

FINAL WORD: *Day 90*

THE BEST DECISION YOU HAVE EVER MADE. . .

To be honest, many of us have come to a place in life, where we had to make decisions on doing things different in order to get the positive results that we so desired for our lives. I have learned that we have the power to do something different once realized we must. If we are not producing positive results in our daily lives, then perhaps, we have not made the best decisions or choices to move us forward. Some would refer to it as being stuck: stuck in our minds, stuck on a job that we dislike, stuck in doing something that amounts to nothing, never realizing our full potential, just settling.

Life does not have to be that way; you can "Reboot" your life. By following a simply and unique strategy, you have chosen to make a difference in your life. You stopped what you were doing, evaluated where you are and re-evaluated where you need to be. You have taken control of your mind, and stopped shifting the responsibility to make decisions for your life on your friends, family, physics or others.

Procrastination is said to be the thief of time. What are you waiting on? Yesterday is gone, and today is the first day of the rest of your new life. So get ready and go! You have made the decision to no more allow fear to keep you from stepping out of the comfort zones you created for yourself.

You have been given strategies, the mind-set, principles, and ways to help you successfully make a decision to have a renewed purpose in life. You have learned six-core elements in how to live a more balanced life, and now living out your fullest potential lies within you. Making a decision to use the 90 day strategic planning tools to reboot your entire way of thinking and non-productive behavioral remedies, has equipped you to get the results you have always desired: "living a life of abundance!"

Is it going to be easy? No, but it is well worth the trip.

Final Word by: *Lady J. Laster*

SPECIAL THANKS & ACKNOWLEDGMENTS

- Angela Bell
- Bishop-Elect Marvin L. Winans, "My Spiritual Father & Friend"
- Brandén L. Newby, "Mr. Genius: thanks for the cover concept"
- Christopher L. Newby, "Home Team!"
- Dr. John E. Newby, "My Eldest Sibling"
- Dr. Nathaniel J. Williams
- Dr. Sabrina Black, "My Mentor & Dear Friend"
- Ellena D. Bennette, "My Big Sis."
- First Lady Evangelist Jacqueline Laster
- Gail Perry-Mason
- God-Made Millionaires
- Lee Newby, "Love You Dad!"
- Mischa Newby
- My Millionaire Mentor: Arthur Cartwright
- Pastor Charles Laster, II, "Thanks for being you!"
- Team Editors *(you know who you are)*
- Tim Feather, Graphics Editor & Designer
- Venus R. Newby

Special
Note of
Thanks!

Many thanks to all for your support. . .

Keep in touch with the author of "Making the Decision to Re-boot Your Life in 90 Days" by sharing your successful: "Life Reboot Story". Your story will be placed as a featured chronicle on Appleseed Professional Development website: www.appleseedpd.com.

Enjoy your future, it is waiting on you!

CREATE YOUR: "Life Reboot Story"

Write your successful "Life Reboot" story! Give
before and after points, strategies and/or techniques
you now implement to maintain daily balance in life
decisions you make.

Date: _____

_____

_____

_____

_____

_____

_____

_____

_____

_____

_____

_____

_____

_____

_____

_____

_____

_____

_____

_____

_____

_____

_____

_____

_____

_____

_____

_____

_____

_____

_____

Notes:

Notes:

_____
_____
_____
_____
_____
_____
_____
_____
_____
_____
_____
_____
_____
_____
_____
_____
_____
_____
_____
_____
_____
_____
_____
_____
_____
_____
_____
_____

References

D. Bender & B. Leon, (1996). Total Fitness.
  Health and Total Fitness, p.55.

Make My Christian Life Work, (2008). Balance Your Life. Retrieved
  August 4, 2010 from the World Wide Web:
  http://www.make-my-christian-life-work.com/balance. html

Meyer, J. (1999, 14 April). I've Got My Mind Made Up. Retrieved
  September 9, 2010 from the World Wide Web:
  http://www.joycemeyer.org/OurMinistries/EverydayAnswers/Articles/art26.htm

W. Manning, E. Keeler, J. Newhouse, E. Sloss, & J. Wasserman,
  1991. Lifestyle, Health & Fitness. Sedentary Lifestyle and
  Chronic Diseases, 52.

Scripture quotations are from: The Holy Bible, New King James
  Version. © 1984 by Thomas Nelson, Inc.

Also Available From Author:

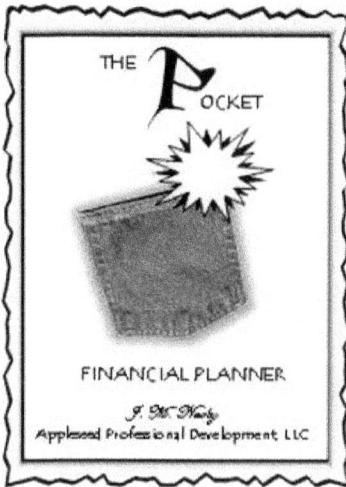

THE POCKET

FINANCIAL PLANNER

J. M. Newby
Appleseed Professional Development LLC

A very simple system to keep track of your daily, weekly and monthly expenses. Conveniently compact so you can carry it along with you, while managing all your daily financial matters.

Includes:
Monthly Calendar
Monthly Budget Worksheets
Weekly Budget Re-caps
Daily Expenditure Sheet
Budgets Tips

Design based on:
Kingdom Building Principles

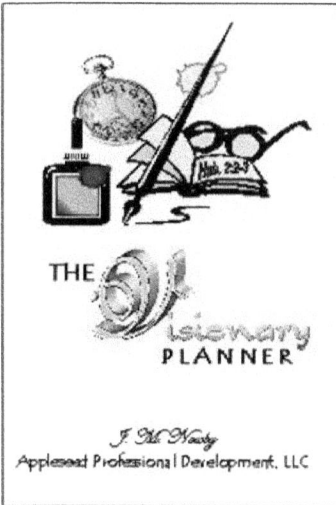

THE Visionary PLANNER

J. M. Newby
Appleseed Professional Development. LLC

An ingenious goal-planning journal constructed to help keep track of daily steps taken towards your destined vision. Conveniently compact, so you can carry it along with you, while maintaining your everyday life endeavors.

Includes:
3 & 5 Year Goal Planning Worksheet
12-month Mapping Process
Daily Journal
Monthly Reflection
Time-Management Activity Log

Designed based on:
Kingdom Building Principles

Coming Soon From Jan M. Newby: "Time To Reboot"™ Journal Series
Time Manager . Financial Management . Day Planner . Fitness & Health Monitor 12-Month Journal . Prayer Journal . Accountability E-News
Stay tuned...